CONTENTS

Bleep & Blorp 2	Amigurumi Friends 26
Groovy Grapes 5	Ned the Narwhal 28
Crabby Patsy 6	Chocolate Pie & Ice Cream 30
Love Monkey 9	Little Piggy 34
Chuck the Groundhog 12	Love My Giraffe 36
Brock the Broccoli 14	Gnome Family 40
Velvet Valentine Bear 18	Squish-a-Saurus 46
Octavia the Octopus 22	Happy Plane, Car & Truck 50

6

12

22

26

30

46

Bleep & Blorp

Easy

MEASUREMENT
Approx 8"/20.5cm long

MATERIALS
Yarn
Bernat® Bundle Up™, 4.9oz/140g balls; each 267yd/244m (polyester) 〔4〕
- 1 ball in #74010 Green Mist or #74023 Posy (A)
- 1 ball in #74001 Marshmallow (B)
- 1 ball in #74022 Dove (C)

Hook
- Size G/6 (4mm) crochet hook, *or size needed to obtain gauge*

Notions
- Stuffing
- Yarn needle

GAUGE
17 hdc and 10 rows = 4"/10cm using size G/6 (4mm) hook. *TAKE TIME TO CHECK GAUGE.*

NOTES
- Ch 2 at beg of rnds does not count as hdc.
- Join all rnds with sl st to first st.

FIRST LEG
**With A, ch 3.
1st rnd: 8 hdc in 3rd ch from hook. Join.
2nd rnd: Ch 2. 2 hdc in each hdc around. Join. 16 hdc.
3rd rnd: Ch 2. *2 hdc in next hdc. 1 hdc in next hdc. Rep from * around. Join. 24 hdc.
4th–6th rnds: Ch 2. 1 hdc in each hdc around. Join.**
Fasten off at end of last rnd.

SECOND LEG
Work from ** to ** as given for First Leg.
Cont as follows for Body:

BODY
Join Legs
1st rnd: With A, ch 2. 1 hdc in each of next 24 hdc of Second Leg. Join with sl st to first hdc. Ch 3. 1 hdc in in each hdc of First Leg. Join with sl st to 1st hdc of First Leg.
2nd rnd: Ch 2. 1 hdc in 1st hdc. 1 hdc in each of next 3 ch. 1 hdc in each of next 24 hdc of Second Leg. 1 hdc in rem loop of each of next 3 ch. 1 hdc in each rem hdc of First Leg. Join. 54 hdc.
3rd–8th rnds: Ch 2. 1 hdc in each hdc around. Join.
9th rnd: Ch 2. *1 hdc in each of next 7 hdc. Hdc2tog. Rep from * around. Join. 48 sts.

10th and 11th rnds: Ch 2. 1 hdc in each st around. Join.

12th rnd: Ch 2. *1 hdc in each of next 6 hdc. Hdc2tog. Rep from * around. Join. 42 sts.

13th and 14th rnds: Ch 2. 1 hdc in each st around. Join.

15th rnd: Ch 2 *1 hdc in each of next 5 hdc. Hdc2tog. Rep from * around. Join. 36 sts.

16th and 17th rnds: Ch 2. 1 hdc in each st around. Join.

18th rnd: Ch 2. *1 hdc in each of next 4 hdc. Hdc2tog. Rep from * around. Join. 30 hdc.

19th rnd: Ch 2. *1 hdc in each of next 3 hdc. Hdc2tog. Rep from * around. Join. 24 hdc.

Fasten off. Stuff Body.

HEAD

With A, ch 3.

1st rnd: 8 hdc in 3rd ch from hook. Join. 8 hdc.

2nd rnd: Ch 2. 2 hdc in each hdc around. Join. 16 hdc.

3rd rnd: Ch 2. *2 hdc in next hdc. 1 hdc in next hdc. Rep from * around. Join. 24 hdc.

4th rnd: Ch 2. *2 hdc in next hdc. 1 hdc in each of next 2 hdc. Rep from * around. Join. 32 hdc.

5th rnd: Ch 2. *2 hdc in next hdc. 1 hdc in each of next 3 hdc. Rep from * around. Join. 40 hdc.

6th rnd: Ch 2. *2 hdc in next hdc. 1 hdc in each of next 4 hdc. Rep from * around. Join. 48 hdc.

7th–14th rnds: Ch 2. 1 hdc in each hdc around. Join.

15th rnd: Ch 2. *Hdc2tog. 1 hdc in each of next 4 hdc. Rep from * around. Join. 40 sts.

16th rnd: Ch 2. *Hdc2tog. 1 hdc in each of next 3 hdc. Rep from * around. Join. 32 sts.

17th rnd: Ch 2. *Hdc2tog. 1 hdc in each of next 2 hdc. Rep from * around. Join. 24 sts. Stuff Head.

18th rnd: Ch 2. *Hdc2tog. 1 hdc in next hdc. Rep from * around. Join. 16 sts.

19th rnd: Ch 2. (Hdc2tog) 8 times.

Fasten off, leaving a long tail. Thread tail through rem sts and draw up tightly. Fasten securely.

Bleep & Blorp

ANTENNAE

With A, ch 3.

1st rnd: 6 hdc in 3rd ch from hook. Join. 6 hdc.

2nd rnd: Ch 2. 2 hdc in each hdc around. Join. 12 hdc.

3rd rnd: Ch 2. *2 hdc in next hdc. 1 hdc in next hdc. Rep from * around. Join. 16 hdc.

4th and 5th rnds: Ch 2. 1 hdc in each hdc around. Join.

6th rnd: Ch 2. *Hdc2tog. 1 hdc in next hdc. Rep from * around. Join. 12 sts.

7th rnd: As 6th rnd. 8 sts. Stuff Antennae.

8th rnd: Ch 1. Working in back loops, 1 sc in each st around. Join.

9th–11th rnds: Ch 1. Working in both loops, 1 sc in each sc around. Join with sl st to 1st sc.

Fasten off at end of last rnd. Stuff rem of Antennae. Sew Antennae to top of Head. Sew Head to top of Body.

ARMS (MAKE 2)

With A, ch 3.

1st rnd: 6 hdc in 3rd ch from hook. Join. 6 hdc.

2nd rnd: Ch 2. 2 hdc in each hdc around. Join. 12 hdc.

3rd–9th rnds: Ch 2. 1 hdc in each hdc around. Join.

10th rnd: Ch 2. *Hdc2tog. 1 hdc in each of next 2 hdc. Rep from * around. Join. 8 sts.

11th–15th rnds: Ch 2. 1 hdc in each st around. Join.

Fasten off at end of last rnd. Stuff Arms lightly. Sew Arms to either side of Body at Neck.

EYE (MAKE 1)

***With B, ch 3.

1st rnd: 8 hdc in 3rd ch from hook. Join. 8 hdc.

2nd rnd: Ch 2. 2 hdc in each hdc around. Join. 16 hdc.***

3rd rnd: Ch 2. *2 hdc in next hdc. 1 hdc in next hdc. Rep from * around. Join. 24 hdc.

4th rnd: Ch 2. *2 hdc in next hdc. 1 hdc in each of next 2 hdc. Rep from * around. Join. 32 hdc.

Fasten off, leaving a long tail to sew Eye to Head.

PUPIL (MAKE 1)

With C, work from *** to *** as given for Eye.

FINISHING

Fasten off, leaving a long tail. Using tail, sew Pupil to Eye as shown in picture. Sew Eye to front of Head as shown in picture. •

Groovy Grapes

Easy

MEASUREMENTS

Approx 9½"/24cm long x 1¾"/4.5cm diameter

MATERIALS

Yarn

Lily® Sugar'n Cream®, 2½oz/71g balls, each approx 120yd/109m (cotton) [4]

Purple Grapes
- 1 ball in #01318 Black Currant (A)
- 1 ball in #01130 Warm Brown (B)

Green Grapes
- 1 ball in #01712 Hot Green (A)
- 1 ball in #01130 Warm Brown (B)

Note: 1 ball of MC will make 22 individual Grapes.

Hook
- Size E/4 (3.5mm) crochet hook, *or size needed to obtain gauge*

Notion
- Stuffing

GAUGE

16 sc and 18 rows = 4"/10cm using size E/4 (3.5mm) hook. *TAKE TIME TO CHECK GAUGE.*

GRAPES (MAKE 15)

With A, ch 2.

1st rnd: 6 sc in 2nd ch from hook. Join with sl st to first sc. 6 sc.

2nd rnd: Ch 1. (2 sc in next sc) 6 times. Join with sl st to first sc. 12 sc.

3rd–5th rnds: Ch 1. 1 sc in each sc around. Join with sl st to first sc.

6th rnd: Ch 1. (Draw up loop in each of next 2 sc. Yoh and draw loop through all loops on hook—sc2tog made) 6 times. Join with sl st to first sc. 6 sts. Fasten off, leaving a long end. Lightly stuff Grape. Thread end through rem sts and draw tightly.

STEM (MAKE 1)

With B, ch 16.

1st row: 1 sc in 2nd ch from hook. 1 sc in each of next 9 ch. Ch 7. 1 sc in 2nd ch from hook. 1 sc in each of next 11 ch. Fasten off.

FINISHING

Sew Grapes to Stem as shown in picture. •

Crabby Patsy

Easy

MEASUREMENTS
Approx 8"/20.5cm wide (including Claws) x 5"/12.5cm tall (including Eyes)

MATERIALS
Yarn

Lily® Sugar'n Cream®, 2½oz/71g balls, each approx 120yd/109m (cotton)
- 1 ball in #00093 Soft Violet, #01712 Hot Green, #00046 Rose Pink, #01740 Hot Pink, #01699 Tangerine (A)
- 1 ball in #00001 White (B)

Hook
- Size G/6 (4mm) crochet hook, *or size needed to obtain gauge*

Notions
- Stuffing
- 4"/10cm square piece of light cardboard
- Piece of black craft felt
- Hot glue gun
- Glue stick

GAUGE
15 sc and 16 rows = 4"/10cm using size G/6 (4mm) hook. *TAKE TIME TO CHECK GAUGE.*

BODY
**With A, ch 7.

1st rnd: 1 sc in 2nd ch from hook. 1 sc in each of next 4 ch. 3 sc in last ch. Do not turn. Working in rem loops of foundation ch, 1 sc in each of next 4 ch. 2 sc in last ch. Join with sl st to first sc. 14 sc.

2nd rnd: Ch 1. 2 sc in first sc. 1 sc in each of next 4 sc. 2 sc in each of next 3 sc. 1 sc in each of next 4 sc. 2 sc in each of next 2 sc. Join with sl st to first sc. 20 sc.

3rd rnd: Ch 1. 1 sc in first sc. 2 sc in next sc. 1 sc in each of next 5 sc. (2 sc in next sc. 1 sc in next sc) 3 times. 1 sc in each of next 4 sc. 2 sc in next sc. 1 sc in next sc. 2 sc in last sc. Join with sl st to first sc. 26 sc.

4th rnd: Ch 1. 1 sc in each of next 2 sc. 2 sc in next sc. 1 sc in each of next 6 sc. (2 sc in next sc. 1 sc in each of next 2 sc) 3 times. 1 sc in each of next 4 sc. 2 sc in next sc. 1 sc in each of next 2 sc. 2 sc in last sc. Join with sl st to first sc. 32 sc.

5th rnd: Ch 1. 1 sc in each of next 3 sc. 2 sc in next sc. 1 sc in each of next 7 sc. (2 sc in next sc. 1 sc in each of next 3 sc) 3 times. 1 sc in each of next 4 sc. 2 sc in next sc. 1 sc in each of next 3 sc. 2 sc in last sc. Join with sl st to first sc. 38 sc.**

6th–9th rnds: Ch 1. 1 sc in each sc around. Join with sl st to first sc. Fasten off at end of 9th rnd.

BASE

Work from ** to ** as given for Body. Fasten off, leaving a long end.
Trace shape of base onto light cardboard. Cut out shape. With end, sew last rnd of Base to last rnd of Body, leaving an opening to insert cardboard base and stuff Body. Sew opening closed.

EYEBALLS (MAKE 2)

With B, ch 2.
1st rnd: 6 sc in 2nd ch from hook. Join with sl st to first sc.
2nd rnd: Ch 1. 2 sc in each sc around. Join with sl st to first sc. 12 sc.

Crabby Patsy

3rd and 4th rnds: Ch 1. 1 sc in each sc around. Join with sl st to first sc.

5th rnd: Ch 1. (Draw up a loop in each of next 2 sts. Yoh and draw through all loops on hook—sc2tog made) 6 times. Stuff eyeball.
Fasten off, leaving a long end. Thread end through rem loops and draw up tightly. Fasten securely.

EYE STEMS (MAKE 2)

***With A, ch 7. Join with sl st to first ch.

1st rnd: Ch 1. 1 sc in each ch around. Join with sl st to first sc. 7 sc.

2nd rnd: Ch 1. 1 sc in each sc around. Join with sl st to first sc. Fasten off.***
Sew Eyeball to top of Stem. Sew Stem to top of Body as shown in picture.

CLAWS (MAKE 2)

With A, ch 2.

1st rnd: 8 sc in 2nd ch from hook. Join with sl st to first sc.

2nd rnd: Ch 1. 2 sc in each sc around. Join with sl st to first sc. 16 sc.

3rd and 4th rnds: Ch 1. *1 sc in next sc. 2 sc in next sc. Rep from * around. 36 sc at end of 4th rnd. Fold piece in half. Ch 1. Working through both thicknesses, 1 sc in each of next 18 sc.
Fasten off.

ARMS (MAKE 2)

Work from *** to *** as given for Eye Stems.
Rep 2nd rnd 3 times more.
Fasten off. Stuff Arms. Sew Claw to end of Arm. Sew Arm to Body as shown in picture.

FINISHING

Cut pupils from black felt. Glue pupils to Eyeballs. •

Love Monkey

Easy

MEASUREMENT
Monkey measures about 7½"/19cm tall.

MATERIALS
Yarn
Red Heart® Super Saver®, 7oz/198g balls, each approx 364yd/215m (acrylic) 4
- 1 ball in #0360 Café Latte (A)
- 1 ball in #0334 Buff (B)
- 1 ball in #0319 Cherry Red (C)
- 1 ball in #0312 Black (D)

Hook
- Size H/8 (5mm) crochet hook, *or size needed to obtain gauge*

Notions
- Yarn needle
- Stitch marker
- One pair 9–12mm safety eyes
- Floral stem wire (optional—to stabilize neck and for pose-able tail)
- Stuffing

GAUGE
16 sts and 16 rnds = 4"/10cm in single crochet using size H/8 (5mm) hook. *TAKE TIME TO CHECK GAUGE.*

STITCH GLOSSARY
reverse sc (reverse single crochet) Work single crochet in opposite direction from which you would usually work (left to right if you are right-handed and right to left if you are left-handed). This stitch is also known as crab stitch. It creates a rope-like twisted single crochet edging.

NOTE
- Gauge is not critical for this project. Work tightly so stuffing will not show through stitches.

HEAD
Beginning at top of head with A, ch 2.

1st rnd: (RS) Work 6 sc in 2nd ch from hook—6 sc. Do not join. Work in continuous rounds (spirals). Place a marker for beginning of round. Move marker up as each round is completed.

2nd rnd: Work 2 sc in each sc around—12 sc.

3rd rnd: [Sc in next sc, 2 sc in next sc] 6 times—18 sc.

4th rnd: [Sc in next 2 sc, 2 sc in next sc] 6 times—24 sc.

5th rnd: [Sc in next 3 sc, 2 sc in next sc] 6 times—30 sc.

6th rnd: [Sc in next 4 sc, 2 sc in next sc] 6 times—36 sc.

7th rnd: [Sc in next 5 sc, 2 sc in next sc] 6 times—42 sc.

8th rnd: [Sc in next 6 sc, 2 sc in next sc] 6 times—48 sc.

Love Monkey

9th–16th rnds: Sc in each sc around.
17th rnd: [Sc in next 6 sc, sc2tog] 6 times—42 sc.
18th rnd: [Sc in next 5 sc, sc2tog] 6 times—36 sc.
19th rnd: [Sc in next 4 sc, sc2tog] 6 times—30 sc.
20th rnd: [Sc in next 3 sc, sc2tog] 6 times—24 sc.
21st rnd: [Sc in next 2 sc, sc2tog] 6 times—18 sc.
22nd rnd: [Sc in next sc, sc2tog] 6 times— 12 sc.
Fasten off, leaving a long tail for sewing head to body.

FACE
Beginning at top of body, with B, ch 2.
1st–4th rnds: Work same as 1st–4th rnds of head—24 sc.
5th rnd: Skip next 2 sc, 9 dc in next sc, skip next 2 sc, sc in next 3 sc, skip next 2 sc, 9 dc in next sc, skip next 2 sc, [sc in next 3 sc, 2 sc in next sc] twice, sc in next 3 sc—34 sts.
6th rnd: 2 sc in next sc, [sc in next 3 sc, 2 sc in next sc] 8 times, sc in last sc—43 sc.
Fasten off, leaving a long tail for sewing face to head. Attach eyes at base of 9-dc groups on 5th rnd. With D and using photograph as a guide, embroider a straight stitch mouth and nose. Sew face to head, sewing around outer edges of face. Stuff head.

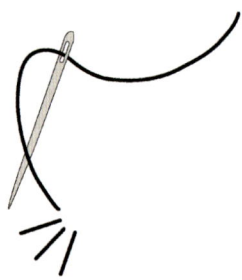
STRAIGHT STITCH

EARS (MAKE 2)
Inner Ear
With B, ch 2.
1st row: Work 5 sc in 2nd ch from hook; do not join, work back and forth in rows, turn—5 sc.
2nd row: Ch 1, 2 sc in each sc across, turn— 10 sc.
3rd row: Ch 1, [sc in next sc, 2 sc in next sc] 5 times, turn—15 sc.
Fasten off.

Outer Ear
With A, work same as inner ear through 3rd row—15 sc. Do not fasten off.
4th row: Ch 1, hold one inner ear and one outer ear together with stitches of last rows matching; working through both thicknesses, sc in each sc across, do not turn.
5th row: Ch 1, reverse sc in each sc across.
Fasten off, leaving a long tail for sewing ear to head. Using photograph as a guide for placement, sew one ear to each side of head.

BODY
Beginning at bottom of body, with A, ch 2.
1st–6th rnds: Work same as 1st–6th rnds of head—36 sc.
7th–14th rnds: Sc in each sc around. Begin stuffing body. Continue to stuff as work progresses.
15th–18th rnds: Work same as 19th–22th rnds of head—12 sc.
Fasten off and weave in ends.

TUMMY HEART
With C, ch 2.
1st row: Sc in 2nd ch from hook, turn—1 sc.
2nd row: Ch 1, 3 sc in the sc, turn—3 sc.
3rd row: Ch 1, 2 sc in first sc, sc in next sc, 2 sc in last sc, turn—5 sc.
4th row: Ch 1, 2 sc in first sc, sc in next 3 sc, 2 sc in last sc, turn—7 sc.
5th row: Ch 1, sc in each sc across, turn.
6th row: Ch 1, 2 sc in first sc, sc in next 5 sc, 2 sc in last sc, turn—9 sc.
7th row: Ch 1, sc in each sc across, turn.
8th row: Skip first 2 sc, 6 dc in next sc, skip next sc, slip st in next sc, skip next sc, 6 dc in next sc, skip last 2 sc, sl st in beginning ch1—13 sts.
Fasten off, leaving a long tail for sewing heart to tummy. Sew heart to front of body. Stuff body.
For additional stability, cut a 10"/25.5cm length of floral stem wire and fold it in half. Insert wire into center of

body, allowing about 2"/5cm to extend from top. Place head on top of body, inserting remainder of wire into center of neck. Sew head to top of body.

ARMS AND LEGS (MAKE A TOTAL OF 4 PIECES—2 FOR ARMS AND 2 FOR LEGS)

Beginning at tip of tail, with A, ch 2.

1st and 2nd rnds: Work same as 1st and 2nd rnds of head—12 sc. No marker is needed for beg of rnd.

3rd–10th rnds: Sc in each sc around.

11th rnd: [Sc in next 4 sc, sc2tog] twice— 10 sc.

12th rnd: Sc in each sc around.

13th rnd: [Sc in next 3 sc, sc2tog] twice—8 sc.

Fasten off, leaving a long tail for sewing limb to body. Stuff limbs lightly and sew to body.

TAIL

With A, ch 2.

1st rnd: (RS) Work 6 sc in 2nd ch from hook—6 sc. Do not join. Work in continuous rounds (spirals). No marker is needed for beginning of round.

2nd rnd: Sc in each sc around. Rep 2nd rnd working until tail measures about 15"/38cm from beginning or desired length.

Fasten off, leaving a long end for sewing tail to body. Stuff tail lightly and sew to back of body.

Note: If a pose-able tail is desired, do not stuff tail. Wrap stuffing around wire, taking special care to wrap around tip of wire, and insert wrapped wire into tail. Leave about 2"/5cm of unwrapped wire extending out of open end of tail. Insert the 2"/5cm end into body before sewing tail in place.

FINISHING

Weave in any remaining ends. •

Chuck the Groundhog

Easy

MEASUREMENT
Approx 4"/10cm tall

MATERIALS
Yarn
Lily® Sugar'n Cream®, 2½oz/71g balls, each approx 120yd/109m (cotton) 4
• 1 ball in #01130 Warm Brown

Hook
• Size E/4 (3.5mm) crochet hook, *or size needed to obtain gauge*

Notions
• 2 small black beads for eyes
• Small amount of black embroidery floss for nose
• Small piece of white felt for teeth
• Stuffing

GAUGE
16 sc and 20 rows = 4"/10cm using size E/4 (3.5mm) hook. *TAKE TIME TO CHECK GAUGE.*

BODY
**With A, ch 2.
1st rnd: 8 sc in 2nd ch from hook. Join with sl st to first sc.
2nd rnd: Ch 1. 2 sc in each sc around. Join with sl st to first sc. 16 sc.
3rd rnd: Ch 1. *1 sc in next sc. 2 sc in next sc. Rep from * around. Join with sl st to first sc. 24 sc.
4th rnd: Ch 1. *1 sc in each of next 2 sc. 2 sc in next sc. Rep from * around. Join with sl st to first sc. 32 sc.
5th rnd: Ch 1. Working in back loops only, 1 sc in each sc around. Join with sl st to first sc.
6th rnd: Ch 1. 1 sc in each sc around. Join with sl st to first sc. Rep last rnd 6 times more.
Note: Stuff Body, then cont stuffing Head as you work shaping.

Head Shaping
1st rnd: Ch 1. *Draw up a loop in each of next 2 sc. Yoh and draw through all loops on hook—sc2tog made. 1 sc in each of next 2 sc. Rep from * around. Join with sl st to first sc. 24 sts.
2nd to 4th rnds: Ch 1. 1 sc in each st around. Join with sl st to first sc.
5th rnd: Ch 1. *Sc2tog over next 2 sc. 1 sc in next sc. Rep from * around. Join with sl st to first sc. 16 sc.
6th to 8th rnds: As 2nd to 4th rnds.
9th rnd: Ch 1. *Sc2tog over next 2 sc. Rep from * around. Join with sl st to first sc. 8 sc.
Fasten off leaving a long end. Draw end tightly through rem sts.

EARS (MAKE 2)
Ch 2.
1st rnd: 6 sc in 2nd ch from hook. Join with sl st to first sc.
2nd rnd: Ch 1. 1 sc in each sc around. Join with sl st to first sc.
Fasten off.

LEGS (MAKE 4)

With A, ch 2.

1st rnd: 8 sc in 2nd ch from hook. Join with sl st to first sc.

2nd to 4th rnds: Ch 1. 1 sc in each sc around. Join with sl st to first sc. Fasten off at end of last rnd.

TAIL

Work as given for Legs.

FINISHING

Attach Ears to top of Head. Stuff Legs and Tail lightly and attach to Body. Sew beads to front of Head for Eyes. With black embroidery floss, embroider nose and mouth. Glue on white felt for teeth. •

Brock the Broccoli

Easy

MEASUREMENTS

Approx 18"/45.5cm tall x 15"/38cm diameter (measured across Large Florette)

MATERIALS

Yarn

Bernat® Baby Blanket™, 10½oz/300g balls, each approx 220yd/201m (polyester) (6)

- 1 ball in #04801 Misty Jungle Green (A)
- 1 ball in #04223 Lemon Lime (B)

Hook

- Size K/10½ (6.5mm) crochet hook, *or size needed to obtain gauge*

Notions

- Split-lock stitch count markers
- 2yd/1.8m black yarn for embroidery
- Steel yarn needles
- Pair of black safety eyes (14mm diameter)
- Stuffing

GAUGE

8 sc and 9 rows = 4"/10cm using size K/10½ (6.5mm) hook. *TAKE TIME TO CHECK GAUGE.*

NOTES

- Join all rnds with sl st to 1st sc.
- Push tr sts to RS of work to create bobbles

LARGE FLORETTE

Beg at top of Large Florette, with A, ch 2.

1st rnd: 8 sc in 2nd ch from hook. Join. 8 sts.

2nd rnd: Ch 1. (1 sc. 1 tr) in each sc around. Join. 16 sts.

3rd rnd: Ch 1. *2 sc in next st. 1 sc in next st. Rep from * around. Join. 24 sts.

4th rnd: Ch 1. *(1 sc. 1 tr) in next sc. 1 sc in next sc. 1 tr in next sc. Rep from * around. Join. 32 sts.

5th rnd: Ch 1. 1 sc in each st around. Join.

6th rnd: Ch 1. *1 sc in next sc. 1 tr in next sc. Rep from * around. Join.

7th rnd: Ch 1. *Sc2tog. 1 sc in each of next 2 sts. Rep from * around. Join. 24 sts.

8th rnd: Ch 1. 2 sc in each sc around. Join. 48 sts.

9th rnd: Ch 1. *1 sc in next sc. 1 tr in next sc. [(1 sc. 1 tr) in next sc] 4 times. 1 sc in next sc. 1 tr in next sc. Rep from * around. Join. 72 sts.

10th rnd: Ch 1. 1 sc in each st around. Join.

11th rnd: Ch 1. *(1 sc in next sc. 1 tr next sc) twice. [(1 sc. 1 tr) in next sc] 4 times. (1 sc in next sc. 1 tr in next sc) twice. Rep from * around. Join. 96 sts.

12th rnd: Ch 1. 1 sc in each st around. Join.

13th rnd: Ch 1. *1 sc in next sc. 1 tr in next sc. Rep from * around. Join.

14th rnd: Ch 1. *1 sc in each of next 4 sts. (Sc2tog) 4 times. 1 sc in each of next 4 sts. Rep from * around. Join. 72 sts.

15th rnd: Ch 1. *1 sc in next sc. 1 tr in next sc. Rep from * around. Join.

16th rnd: Ch 1. *1 sc in each of next 2 sts. (Sc2tog) 4 times. 1 sc in each of next 2 sts. Rep from * around. Join. 48 sts.

17th rnd: Ch 1. *1 sc in next sc. 1 tr in next sc. Rep from * around. Join.

18th rnd: Ch 1. *Sc2tog. 1 sc in each of next 2 sts. Rep from * around. Join. 36 sts. Fasten off.

SMALL FLORETTE

With A, ch 2.

1st rnd: 8 sc in 2nd ch from hook. Join. 8 sts.

2nd rnd: Ch 1. (1 sc. 1 tr) in each sc around. Join. 16 sts.

Brock the Broccoli

3rd rnd: Ch 1. *2 sc in next st. 1 sc in next st. Rep from * around. Join. 24 sts.

4th rnd: Ch 1. *1 sc in next sc. 1 tr in next sc. Rep from * around. Join.

5th rnd: Ch 1. 1 sc in each sc around. Join.

6th rnd: Ch 1. *1 sc in next sc. 1 tr in next sc. Rep from * around. Join.

7th rnd: Ch 1. *Sc2tog. 1 sc in next sc. Join. 12 sc. Fasten off.

STEM

Note: Stem is worked in a continuous spiral. Do not join at end of rnds. Place marker on 1st stitch of rnd and move marker each rnd to keep place.

With B, ch 2.

1st rnd: 8 sc in 2nd ch from hook. Do not join. 8 sc.

2nd rnd: 2 sc in each sc around. 16 sc.

3rd rnd: *2 sc in next sc. 1 sc in next sc. Rep from * around. 24 sc.

4th rnd: *2 sc in 1st sc. 1 sc in each of next 2 sc. Rep from * around. 32 sc.

5th rnd: *2 sc in 1st sc. 1 sc in each of next 3 sc. Rep from * around. 40 sc.

6th rnd: Working in back loops only, 1 sc in each sc around.

7th rnd: Working in both loops, 1 sc in each sc around.

8th to 11th rnds: 1 sc in each sc around.

12th rnd: *Sc2tog. 1 sc in each of next 8 sc. Rep from * around. 36 sc.

13th rnd: 1 sc in each sc around.

14th rnd: *1 sc in each of next 3 sc. Sc2tog. 1 sc in each of next 4 sc. Rep from * around. 32 sts.

15th and 16th rnds: 1 sc in each sc around.

17th rnd (Branch opening): 1 sc in each of 1st 6 sc. Ch 4. Skip next 8 sc. 1 sc in next sc and each sc to end of rnd. 32 sts (including ch-4).

18th rnd: 1 sc in each sc and ch to end of rnd. 32 sts.

19th rnd: *2 sc in next sc. 1 sc in each of next 7 sc. Rep from * around. 36 sts.

20th and 21st rnds: 1 sc in each sc and ch to end of rnd.

22nd rnd: 1 sc in each sc around. Sl st in 1st sc of next rnd. Fasten off.

BRANCH

Note: Branch is worked in a continuous spiral. Do not join at end of rnds. Place marker on 1st stitch of rnd and move marker each rnd to keep place.

Join B with sl st to 1st skipped st from 17th rnd of Stem.

1st rnd: Ch 1. 1 sc in each of next 8 sc. Working across opposite side of ch 4, 1 sc in each of next 4 ch. Join with sl st to 1st sc. 12 sc.

2nd to 4th rnds: 1 sc in each sc around.

5th rnd: 1 sc in each sc around. Sl st in 1st sc of next rnd. Fasten off.

FINISHING

Attach safety eyes to Stem as shown in photo. Stuff Large and Small Florettes, Stem and Branch. Sew last rnd of Stem and last rnd of Large Florette tog. Sew last rnd of Branch and last rnd of Small Florette tog. With black yarn, embroider mouth using straight st as seen in photo. •

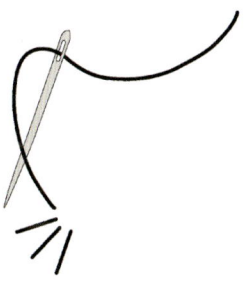

STRAIGHT STITCH

Velvet Valentine Bear

Designed by Sarah Zimmerman (Repeat Crafter Me)

Easy

MEASUREMENT
Approx 11"/28cm tall

MATERIALS
Yarn
Bernat® Velvet™, 10½oz/300g balls; each 315yd/288m (polyester) [5]
- 1 ball in #32017 Terracotta Rose (A)
- 1 ball in #32013 Quiet Pink (B)

Hook
- Size H/8 (5mm) crochet hook, *or size needed to obtain gauge*

Notions
- 9mm safety eyes
- Black safety nose
- Stuffing
- Yarn needle

GAUGE
12 sc and 12 rows = 4"/10cm using size H/8 (5mm) hook. *TAKE TIME TO CHECK GAUGE.*

SPECIAL TECHNIQUE
Magic loop Wrap yarn into a ring, ensuring that tail falls behind working yarn. Pinch ring and tail between middle finger and thumb. Insert hook through center of ring, yoh (with working yarn) and draw up a loop. Work stitches of first round in ring. After first round of stitches is worked, pull gently on tail to tighten ring.

BODY
With A, begin using magic loop method.
1st rnd: Ch 1. 10 sc in magic loop. Join with sl st to first sc.
2nd rnd: Ch 1. 2 sc in each st around. Join with sl st to first sc. 20 sc.
3rd rnd: Ch 1. 1 sc in each st around. Join with sl st to first sc.
4th rnd: Ch 1. 2 sc in first sc. *1 sc in next sc. 2 sc in next sc. Rep from * to last st. 1 sc in last sc. Join with sl st to first sc. 30 sc.
5th—11th rnds: As 3rd rnd.
12th rnd: Ch 1. *Sc2tog. 1 sc in each of next 4 sc. Rep from * around. Join with sl st to first sc. 25 sc.
13th rnd: As 3rd rnd.
14th rnd: Ch 1. *Sc2tog. 1 sc in each of next 3 sc. Rep from * around. Join with sl st to first sc. 20 sc.
15th rnd: As 3rd rnd.
16th rnd: Ch 1. *Sc2tog. 1 sc in each of next 2 sc. Rep from * around. Join with sl st to first sc. 15 sc.
17th–19th rnds: As 3rd rnd.
Fasten off, leaving a long tail. Stuff, leaving top open.

SNOUT
With B, ch 5.
1st rnd: 1 sc in 2nd ch from hook. 1 sc in each of next 2 ch. 2 sc in next ch. Working into opposite side of ch, 1 sc in each of next 3 ch. 2 sc in last ch. Join with sl st to first sc. 10 sc.
2nd rnd: Ch 1. 2 sc in each sc around. Join with sl st to first sc. 20 sc.

Velvet Valentine Bear

3rd rnd: Ch 1. 1 sc in each sc around. Join with sl st to first sc.

Fasten off, leaving a long tail. Add safety nose, as pictured.

HEAD

With A, begin using magic loop.

1st rnd: Ch 1. 8 sc in magic loop. Join with sl st to first sc.

2nd rnd: Ch 1. 2 sc in each sc around. Join with sl st to first st. 16 sc.

3rd rnd: Ch 1. 2 sc in first sc. *1 sc in next sc. 2 sc in next sc. Rep from * to last st. 1 sc in last sc. Join with sl st to first sc. 24 sc.

4th rnd: Ch 1. 2 sc in first sc. *1 sc in each of next 2 sc. 2 sc in next sc. Rep from * to last st. 1 sc in last sc. Join with sl st to first sc. 32 sc.

5th rnd: Ch 1. 2 sc in first sc. *1 sc in each of next 3 sc. 2 sc in next sc. Rep from * to last st. 1 sc in last sc. Join with sl st to first sc. 40 sc.

6th–13th rnds: Ch 1. 1 sc in each st. around. Join with sl st to first sc.

14th rnd: Ch 1. *Sc2tog. 1 sc in each of next 3 sc. Rep from * around. Join with sl st to first sc. 32 sc.

15th rnd: As 6th rnd.

16th rnd: Ch 1. *Sc2tog. 1 sc in each of next 2 sc. Rep from * around. Join with sl st to first sc. 24 sc.

17th rnd: As 6th rnd.

18th rnd: Ch 1. *Sc2tog. 1 sc in next sc. Rep from * around. Join with sl st to first sc. 16 sc.

19th rnd: As 6th rnd. Sew on snout, stuffing lightly as you work. Attach safety eyes.

20th rnd: Ch 1. *Sc2tog. 1 sc in each of next 2 sc. Rep from * around. Join with sl st to first sc. 12 sc.

21st rnd: Ch 1. *Sc2tog. Rep from * around. Join with sl st to first sc.

Fasten off leaving a long end. Draw end tightly through rem sts and fasten securely.

ARMS (MAKE 2)

With A, begin using magic loop.

1st rnd: Ch 1. 10 sc in magic loop. Work in continuous rnds without joining with sl st, and omitting starting ch at beg of rnd.

2nd–7th rnds: 1 sc in each sc around.

8th rnd: (Sc2tog. 1 sc in each of next 3 sc) twice.

9th–14th rnds: As 2nd—7th rnds.

Fasten off, leaving a long tail. Stuff.

EARS (MAKE 2)

With A, begin using magic loop.

1st rnd: Ch 1. 5 sc in magic loop. Join with sl st to first sc.

2nd rnd: Ch 1. 2 sc in each sc around. Join with sl st to first sc. 10 sc.

3rd rnd: Ch 1. 2 sc in next sc. *1 sc in next sc. 2 sc in next sc. Rep from * to last sc. 1 sc in last sc. Join with sl st to first sc. 15 sc.

4th rnd: Ch 1. 1 sc in each sc around. Join with sl st to first sc.

5th rnd: Ch 1. *Sc2tog. 1 sc in next sc. Rep from * around. Join with sl st to first sc. 10 sc.

Fasten off, leaving a long tail. Sew ears to head.

FEET (MAKE 2)

With B, begin using magic loop.

1st rnd: Ch 1. 6 sc in magic loop. Join with sl st to first sc.

2nd rnd: Ch 2. 2 dc in each of first 2 sts. 2 hdc in next st. 2 sc in each of next 2 sts. 2 hdc in last st. Join with sl st to first dc. 12 sts.

3rd rnd: Ch 1. 2 sc in first st. *1 sc in next sc. 2 sc in next sc. Rep from * to last st. 1 sc in last st. Join with sl st to first sc. 18 sc. Break B. Join A.

4th–5th rnds: Ch 1. 1 sc in each sc around. Join with sl st to first sc.

6th rnd: Ch 1. (Sc2tog) 4 times. 1 sc in each of next

10 sts. Join with sl st to first sc. 14 sc.

7th rnd: Ch 1. (Sc2tog) twice. 1 sc in each of next
10 sts. Join with sl st to first sc. 12 sc.

8th—9th rnds: As 4th and 5th rnds.
Fasten off. Stuff and sew to bottom of Body as pictured.

TAIL

With A, begin using magic loop.

1st rnd: Ch 1. 6 sc in magic loop. Join with sl st to
first sc.

2nd rnd: Ch 1. 2 sc in each sc around. Join with sl st to first sc. 12 sc.

3rd rnd: Ch 1. 1 sc in each sc around. Join with sl st to first sc.

4th rnd: Ch 1. *Sc2tog. 1 sc in next sc. Rep from * around. Join with sl st to first sc. 8 sc.

Fasten off, leaving a long tail. Stuff and sew to back of Body as pictured

EASY HEART PATTERN

With B, ch 7.

1st row: 1 sc in 2nd ch from hook. 1 sc in each ch to end of ch. 6 sc. Turn.

2nd row: Ch 1. 1 sc in each sc to end of row. Turn.

3rd row: As 2nd row.

4th–6th rows: Ch 1. 1 sc in each of next 3 sts. Turn.

7th row: Ch 1. 1 sc in each of next 3 sts. Do not turn. Work 1 rnd of sc evenly around entire perimeter of heart, working (Sc. Ch 1. Sc) into bottom stitch, where slip knot is located. Join with sl st to first sc of 7th row.

FINISHING

Fasten off. Sew to Body as pictured. •

Octavia the Octopus

Easy

MEASUREMENT
Approx 7"/18cm tall

MATERIALS
Yarn

Lily® Sugar'n Cream®, 2½oz/71g balls, each approx 120yd/109m (cotton) [4]

- 2 balls in #00071 Grape or #01628 Hot Orange (A)
- 2 balls in #00002 Black or #01130 Warm Brown (B)
- 1 ball in #00001 White (C)

Hook

- Size G/6 (4mm) crochet hook, *or size needed to obtain gauge*

Notion

- Stuffing

GAUGE
15 sc and 16 rows = 4"/10cm using size G/6 (4mm) hook. *TAKE TIME TO CHECK GAUGE.*

HEAD
With A, ch 2.

**1st rnd: 7 sc in 2nd ch from hook. Join with sl st to first sc. 7 sc.

2nd rnd: Ch 1. 2 sc in each sc around. Join with sl st to first sc. 14 sc.

3rd rnd: Ch 1. *1 sc in next sc. 2 sc in next sc. Rep from * around. Join with sl st to first sc. 21 sc.

4th rnd: Ch 1. *1 sc in each of next 2 sc. 2 sc in next sc. Rep from * around. Join with sl st to first sc. 28 sc.

5th rnd: Ch 1. *1 sc in each of next 3 sc. 2 sc in next sc. Rep from * around. Join with sl st to first sc. 35 sc.

6th rnd: Ch 1. *1 sc in each of next 4 sc. 2 sc in next sc. Rep from * around. Join with sl st to first sc. 42 sc.**

7th and alt rnds: Ch 1. 1 sc in each sc around. Join with sl st to first sc.

8th rnd: Ch 1. *1 sc in each of next 5 sc. 2 sc in next sc. Rep from * around. Join with sl st to first sc. 49 sc.

10th rnd: Ch 1. *1 sc in each of next 6 sc. 2 sc in next sc. Rep from * around. Join with sl st to first sc. 56 sc.

12th rnd: Ch 1. *1 sc in each of next 7 sc. 2 sc in next sc. Rep from * around. Join with sl st to first sc. 63 sc.

13th to 17th rnds: Ch 1. 1 sc in each sc around. Join with sl st to first sc.

18th rnd: Ch 1. *1 sc in each of next 7 sc. Sc2tog. Rep from * around. Join with sl st to first sc. 56 sts.

19th and 20th rnds: Ch 1. 1 sc in each sc around. Join with sl st to first sc.

21st rnd: Ch 1. *1 sc in each of next 6 sc. Sc2tog. Rep from * around. Join with sl st to first sc. 49 sts.

22nd and 23rd rnds: Ch 1. 1 sc in each sc around. Join with sl st to first sc.

24th rnd: Ch 1. *1 sc in each of next 5 sc. Sc2tog. Rep from * around. Join with sl st to first sc. 42 sts.

25th and 26th rnds: Ch 1. 1 sc in each sc around. Join with sl st to first sc.

27th rnd: Ch 1. *1 sc in each of next 4 sc. Sc2tog. Rep from * around. Join with sl st to first sc. 35 sts.

28th–30th rnds: Ch 1. 1 sc in each sc around. Join with sl st to first sc.

31st rnd: Ch 1. *1 sc in each of next 6 sc. 2 sc in next sc. Rep from * around. Join with sl st to first sc. 40 sc.

32nd rnd: Ch 1. *1 sc in each of next 4 sc. 2 sc in next sc. Rep from * around. Join with sl st to first sc. 48 sc.

33rd rnd: Ch 1. *1 sc in each of next 5 sc. 2 sc in next sc. Rep from * around. Join with sl st to first sc. 56 sc.

34th rnd: Ch 1. *1 sc in each of next 6 sc. 2 sc in next sc. Rep from * around. 64 sc.

35th rnd: Ch 1. *1 sc in each of next 7 sc. 2 sc in next sc. Rep from * around. 72 sc.

Octavia the Octopus

Divide for Tentacles

Note: Ch 2 at beg of row does not count as st.

***1st row: Ch 2. Hdc2tog. 1 hdc in each of next 5 sc. Hdc2tog. Turn. Leave rem sts unworked.

2nd and 3rd rows: Ch 2. 1 hdc in each of next 7 sts. Turn.

4th row: Ch 2. Hdc2tog. 1 hdc in each of next 3 hdc. Hdc2tog. Turn.

5th and 6th rows: Ch 2. 1 hdc in each of next 5 sts. Turn.

7th row: Ch 2. 1 hdc in first hdc. Hdc2tog. 1 hdc in each of next 2 hdc. Turn. 4 sts.

8th row: Ch 34. 3 sc in 2nd ch from hook. (1 sc in next ch. 2 sc in next ch) 4 times. (1 hdc in next ch. 2 hdc in next ch) 4 times. (1 dc in next ch. 2 dc in next ch) 4 times. (1 tr in next ch. 2 tr in next ch) 4 times. Skip 3 hdc of 7th row. Sl st to top of last hdc. Fasten off.***

****Join A with sl st to next missed sc of last rnd. Rep from *** to *** as before. ****

Rep from **** to **** 6 times more.

BOTTOM

With B, rep from ** to ** as given for Head.

7th rnd: *Ch 1. 1 sc in each of next 5 sc. 2 sc in next sc. Rep from * around. 49 sc. Join with sl st to first sc.

8th and 9th rnds: *Ch 1. 1 sc in each of next 6 sc. 2 sc in next sc. Rep from * around. Join with sl st to first sc. 64 sc at end of last rnd.

10th rnd: *Ch 1. 1 sc in each of next 7 sc. 2 sc in next sc. Rep from * around. Join with sl st to first sc. 72 sc. Work from *** to *** as given for Tentacles.

Rep from **** to **** 6 times more as given for Tentacles.

EYES (MAKE 2)

With B, ch 2.

**1st rnd: 6 sc in 2nd ch from hook. Join with sl st to first sc.

2nd rnd: With B, ch 1. 2 sc in each sc around. Join C with sl st to first sc.

3rd rnd: With C, ch 1. *2 sc in next sc. 1 sc in next sc. Rep from * around. Join with sl st to first sc.

4th–6th rnds: Ch 1. 1 sc in each sc around. Join with sl st to first sc.**

7th rnd: Ch 1. *1 sc in next sc. Sc2tog. Rep from * around.

8th rnd: Ch 1. Sc2tog. Rep from * around. Break C, leaving a long end. Stuff Eye. Thread yarn through rem sts pull tightly and fasten securely.

EYELIDS (MAKE 2)

With A, work from ** to ** as given for Eye. Fasten off. Insert Eye into Eyelid. Sew each Eye to body of Octopus as shown in picture.

FINISHING

Stuff Head. Align tentacles of Head with tentacles of Bottom. With WS of Head and RS of Tentacles tog, join C at beg of tentacle at longer side. Working through both thickessess, 1 sc in each st along longer sides of tentacle of to turning ch 1. Fasten off. With B, sew shorter sides of tentacle (tentacle will curl by itself). Rep for all tentacles. Sew Eyes in position, as shown in picture. •

Amigurumi Friends

●● Easy

MEASUREMENT
Approx 4"/10cm tall, excluding Legs and Ears

MATERIALS
Yarn
Caron® Little Crafties™, 0.7oz/20g; each 63yd/58 (acrylic) per shade (Each package includes 20 shades.)
- 1 ball in Orchid (Rabbit)
- 1 ball in Icy Teal (Mouse)
- 1 ball in Lemon (Cat)
- Small amount of Black for Nose and Eyes embroidery

Hook
- Size G/6 (4mm) crochet hook, *or size needed to obtain gauge*

Notions
- Yarn needle
- Stuffing

GAUGE
17 sc and 21 rows = 4"/10cm using size G/6 (4mm) hook. *TAKE TIME TO CHECK GAUGE.*

NOTE
- Join all rnds with sl st to 1st sc.

BODY (ALL VERSIONS)
Ch 2.

1st rnd: 6 sc in 2nd ch from hook. Join. 6 sc.

2nd rnd: Ch 1. 2 sc in each sc around. Join. 12 sc.

3rd rnd: Ch 1. *1 sc in next sc. 2 sc in next sc. Rep from * around. Join. 18 sc.

4th rnd: Ch 1. *1 sc in each of next 2 sc. 2 sc in next sc. Rep from * around. Join. 24 sc.

5th–18th rnds: Ch 1. 1 sc in each sc around. Join.

19th rnd: Ch 1. *1 sc in each of next 2 sc. Sc2tog. Rep from * around. Join. 18 sc. Stuff Body firmly.

20th rnd: Ch 1. *1 sc in next sc. Sc2tog. Rep from * around. Join. 12 sc.

21st rnd: Ch 1. *Sc2tog. Rep from * around. Join. 6 sc. Fasten off, leaving a long end. Draw end tightly through rem sts.

LEGS (MAKE 2; ALL VERSIONS)
Ch 2.

1st rnd: 6 sc in 2nd ch from hook. Join. 6 sc.

2nd rnd: Ch 1. Working in back loops only, 1 sc in each sc around. Join.

3rd rnd: Ch 1. 1 sc in each sc around. Join. Fasten off, leaving a long end for joining. Sew Legs to bottom of Body as shown in photo.

ARMS (MAKE 2; ALL VERSIONS)

Ch 2.

1st rnd: 6 sc in 2nd ch from hook. Join. 6 sc.

2nd rnd: Ch 1. Working in back loops only, 1 sc in each sc around. Join.

3rd–5th rnds: Ch 1. 1 sc in each sc around. Join. Fasten off, leaving a long end for joining. Sew Arms to side of Body as shown in photo.

RABBIT EARS (MAKE 2)

Ch 5.

1st row: 1 sc in 2nd ch from hook. 1 sc in each of next 2 ch. 4 sc in last ch. Working in opposite side of foundation ch, 1 sc in each of next 3 ch. Fasten off. Sew Ears to top of Body as shown in photo.

MOUSE EARS (MAKE 2)

Ch 2.

1st rnd: 6 sc in 2nd ch from hook. Join. 6 sc.

2nd rnd: Ch 1. 2 sc in each sc around. Join. 12 sc. Fasten off. Sew Ears to top of Body as shown in photo.

CAT EARS (MAKE 2)

Ch 4.

1st row: 1 sc in 2nd ch from hook. 1 sc in each ch to end of row. Turn. 3 sc.

2nd row: Ch 1. Sc3tog.

Fasten off. Sew Ears to top of Body as shown in photo.

FINISHING

With 10"/25.5cm strand of Black, embroider Eyes using French Knot and Nose using Satin Stitch as shown in photos. •

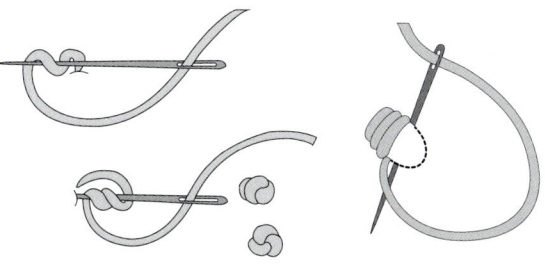

FRENCH KNOT STITCH   **SATIN STITCH**

Ned the Narwhal

Easy

MEASUREMENT
Approx 21"/53.5cm long

MATERIALS
Yarn
Lily® Sugar'n Cream®, 2½oz/71g balls, each approx 120yd/109m (cotton) 4
- 2 balls in #01133 Teal (A)
- 1 ball in #01004 Soft Ecru (B)
- 1 ball in #00002 Black (C)

Hook
- Size H/8 (5mm) crochet hook, *or size needed to obtain gauge*

Notion
- Stuffing

GAUGE
13 sc and 14 rows = 4"/10cm using size H/8 (5mm) hook. *TAKE TIME TO CHECK GAUGE.*

NOTE
- Join all rnds with sl st to first sc. Turn at end of each rnd, alternating RS and WS throughout.

BODY
With A, ch 2.
1st rnd: (RS). 6 sc in 2nd ch from hook. Join. Turn. 6 sc.
2nd rnd: (WS). Ch 1. 2 sc in each sc around. Join. Turn. 12 sc.
3rd rnd: Ch 1. *1 sc in next sc. 2 sc in next sc. Rep from * around. Join. Turn. 18 sc.
4th rnd: Ch 1. *1 sc in each of next 2 sc. 2 sc in next sc. Rep from * around. Join. Turn. 24 sc.
5th rnd: Ch 1. *1 sc in each of next 3 sc. 2 sc in next sc. Rep from * around. Join. Turn. 30 sc.
6th rnd: Ch 1. *1 sc in each of next 4 sc. 2 sc in next sc. Rep from * around. Join. Turn. 36 sc.
7th rnd: Ch 1. *1 sc in each of next 5 sc. 2 sc in next sc. Rep from * around. Join. Turn. 42 sc.
8th–11th rnds: Ch 1. 1 sc in each sc around. Join. Turn.
12th rnd: Ch 1. 1 sc in each of next 19 sc. 2 sc in each of next 4 sc. 1 sc in each sc of last 19 sc. Join. Turn. 46 sc.
13th–30th rnds: Ch 1. 1 sc in each sc around. Join. Turn.
31st rnd: Ch 1. 1 sc in each of next 19 sc. (Sc2tog) 4 times. 1 sc in each of last 19 sc. Join. Turn. 36 sc.
32nd–34th rnds: Ch 1. 1 sc in each sc around. Join. Turn. Stuff Body.

TAIL
35th rnd: Ch 1. (Sc2tog) 3 times. 1 sc in each sc to last 6 sc. (Sc2tog) 3 times. Join. Turn.
36th rnd: Ch 1. 1 sc in each sc around. Join. Turn.
37th–42nd rnds: Rep last 2 rnds 3 times more.
43rd–46th rnds: Ch 1. 1 sc in each sc around. Join. Turn.
47th rnd: Ch 1. 1 sc in each of next 4 sc. 2 sc in next sc. 1 sc in each of next 8 sc. 2 sc in next sc. 1 sc in each of last 4 sc. Join. Turn. 20 sc.
48th rnd: Ch 1. 1 sc in each of next 4 sc. 2 sc in each of next 2 sc. 1 sc in each of next 8 sc. 2 sc in each of next 2 sc. 1 sc in each of last 4 sc. Join. Turn. 24 sc.
49th rnd: Ch 1. 1 sc in each of next 5 sc. 2 sc in each of next 2 sc. 1 sc in each of next 10 sc. 2 sc in each of next 2 sc. 1 sc in each of last 5 sc. Join. Turn. 28 sc.
50th rnd: Ch 1. 1 sc in each of next 6 sc. 2 sc in each of next 2 sc. 1 sc in each of next 12 sc. 2 sc in each of next 2 sc. 1 sc in each of last 6 sc. Join. Turn. 32 sc.

51st rnd: Ch 1. 1 sc in each of next 7 sc. 2 sc in each of next 2 sc. 1 sc in each of next 14 sc. 2 sc in each of next 2 sc. 1 sc in each of last 7 sc. Join. Turn. 36 sc.

52nd rnd: Ch 1. 1 sc in each of next 8 sc. 2 sc in each of next 2 sc. 1 sc in each of next 8 sc. Skip last 18 sts. Join. Turn. 20 sc.

**53rd rnd: Ch 1. 1 sc in each sc around. Join. Turn.

54th rnd: Ch 1. Sc2tog. 1 sc in each sc to last 2 sc. Sc2tog. Join. Turn. 18 sc.

55th rnd: Ch 1. 1 sc in each sc around. Join. Turn.

56th rnd: Ch 1. Sc2tog. 1 sc in each sc to last 2 sc. Sc2tog. Join. Turn. 16 sc.

57th rnd: Ch 1. (Sc2tog) 3 times. 1 sc in each of next 4 sc. Sc2tog 3 times. Join. Turn. 10 sc. Stuff Tail.

58th rnd: Ch 1. (Sc2tog) 5 times. Join. 5 sc. Fasten off, leaving a long end. Draw end tightly through rem sts.**

Next rnd: With WS facing, join A to last skipped st in 52nd rnd. 1 sc in each of next 8 sc. 2 sc in each of next 2 sc. 1 sc in each of next 8 sc. Join. Turn. 20 sc. Rep from ** to **.

TUSK

With B, ch 8. Join with sl st to first ch, making sure not to twist ch.

Note: Do not turn at end of rnds while working Tusk.

1st rnd: Ch 1. 1 sc in each ch around. Join. 8 sc.

2nd–8th rnds: Ch 1. 1 sc in each sc around. Join.

9th rnd: Ch 1. (1 sc in each of next 2 sc. Sc2tog) twice. Join. 6 sc.

10th–15th rnds: Ch 1. 1 sc in each sc around. Join. Fasten off, leaving a long end. Draw end tightly through rem sts.

FLIPPERS (MAKE 2)

With A, ch 4.

1st row: 1 sc in 2nd ch from hook. 1 sc in each ch to end of row. Turn. 3 sc.

2nd row: Ch 1. 2 sc in next sc. 1 sc in next sc. 2 sc in last sc. Turn. 5 sts.

3rd–6th rows: Ch 1. 1 sc in each sc to end of row. Turn. Do not fasten off. Do not turn.

Flipper Edging

Ch 1. Work sc evenly around sides and ch edge. Fasten off.

FINISHING

Sew Tusk and Flippers onto Body as shown in picture. With C, embroider Eyes with satin stitch as shown in picture. •

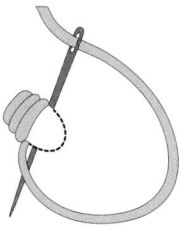

SATIN STITCH

Chocolate Pie & Ice Cream

Easy

MEASUREMENTS
Pie is 4½"/11.5cm from point to back of crust. Ice Cream is 8"/20cm long.

MATERIALS
Yarn
Red Heart® Super Saver®, 7oz/198g balls, each approx 364yd/215m (acrylic)
- 1 ball in #0334 Buff (A)
- 1 ball in #0365 Coffee (B)
- 1 ball in #0316 Soft White (C)

Hook
- Size E/4 (3.5mm) crochet hook, *or size needed to obtain gauge*

Notions
- Stuffing
- Split-ring stitch marker
- Yarn needle

GAUGE
13 sc and 16 rows = 4"/10cm using size E/4 (3.5mm) hook. *TAKE TIME TO CHECK GAUGE.*

NOTE
- When working in rounds do not join or turn; instead, place marker to indicate 1st st of round, and work continuously.

CHOCOLATE PIE
Crust
With A, ch 2.

1st row: 3 sc in 2nd ch from hook; turn—3 sts.

2nd row: Ch 1, sc in each st across; turn.

3rd row: Ch 1, 2 sc in 1st st, sc to last st, 2 sc in last st; turn—5 sts.

4th–15th rows: Rep 2nd and 3rd rows—17 sts at end of 15th row.

16th row: Rep 2nd row.

17th row: Ch 1, working in back loops ONLY, sc in each st across; turn.

18th–21st rows: Rep 2nd row.

22nd row: Ch 1, (sc, dc, sc) all in 1st st; * slip st in next st, (sc, dc, sc) all in next st; rep from * across. Fasten off.

Chocolate
With B, work same as Crust through 16th row.

17th row: Ch 1, sc in each st across; DO NOT TURN; work 16 sc evenly along edge, 1 sc in tip, 16 sc evenly along other edge; turn—50 sts.

18th row: Ch 1, working in front loops ONLY, sc in first 33 sts; turn.

19th row: Working in these 33 sts only, ch 1, sc in each st across; turn.

20th and 21st rows: Rep 19th row. Fasten off.

Join: Hold Chocolate in place on Crust and attach A in top back left corner of Crust. Ch 1, work through both Chocolate and Crust, sc evenly down side, across bottom edge, and up other side.
Fasten off. Stuff pie and with A, sew opening closed.

Whipped Cream
With C, ch 30.

1st row: 3 dc in 3rd ch from hook and in next 14 ch, 3 tr in remaining ch across.

Chocolate Pie & Ice Cream

FINISHING

Fasten off. Curl Whipped Cream according to photo and sew to top of Pie.

ICE CREAM CONE

Cone

With A, ch 2.

1st rnd: 6 sc in 2nd ch from hook.

2nd rnd: * Sc in next 2 sts, 2 sc in next st; rep from * around—8 sts.

3rd rnd: * Sc in next 3 sts, 2 sc in next st; rep from * around—10 sts.

4th rnd: * Sc in next 4 sts, 2 sc in next st; rep from * around—12 sts.

5th rnd: * Sc in next 5 sts, 2 sc in next st; rep from * around—14 sts.

6th rnd: * Sc in next 6 sts, 2 sc in next st; rep from * around—16 sts.

7th rnd: * Sc in next 7 sts, 2 sc in next st; rep from * around—18 sts.

8th rnd: * Sc in next 8 sts, 2 sc in next st; rep from * around—20 sts.

9th rnd: * Sc in next 9 sts, 2 sc in next st; rep from * around—22 sts.

10th rnd: Sc in each st around.

11th rnd: * Sc in next 10 sts, 2 sc in next st; rep from * around—24 sts.

12th rnd: Rep 10th rnd.

13th rnd: * Sc in next 11 sts, 2 sc in next st; rep from * around—26 sts.

14th rnd: Rep 10th rnd.

15th rnd: * Sc in next 12 sts, 2 sc in next st; rep from * around—28 sts.

16th rnd: Rep 10th rnd.

17th rnd: * Sc in next 13 sts, 2 sc in next st; rep from * around—30 sts.

18th rnd: Rep   .

Fasten off.

Ice Cream

With C, ch 2.

1st row: Sc in 2nd ch from hook; turn—1 st.

2nd row: Ch 1, sc in st; turn.

3rd row: Ch 1, 2 sc in st; turn—2 sts.

4th row: Ch 1, sc in each st across; turn.

5th row: Ch 1, sc in 1st st, 2 sc in next st; turn—3 sts.

6th row: Rep 4th row.

7th row: Ch 1, sc in 1st st, 2 sc in next st, sc in next st; turn—4 sts.

8th row: Ch 1, sc in 1st st, 2 sc in next st, sc in remaining sts; turn—5 sts.

9th row: Ch 1, sc in 1st 2 sts, 2 sc in next st, sc in remaining sts; join with a slip st to first sc to form ring, begin working in rounds—6 sts.

10th rnd: * 2 sc in next st; rep from * around—12 sts.

11th rnd: * Sc in next st, 2 sc in next st; rep from * around—18 sts.

12th rnd: * Sc in next 2 sts, 2 sc in next st; rep from * around—24 sts.

13th rnd: Sc in each st around.

14th rnd: * Sc in next 3 sts, 2 sc in next st; rep from * around—30 sts.

15th rnd: * Sc in next 4 sts, 2 sc in next st; rep from * around—36 sts.

16th rnd: Rep 13th rnd.

17th rnd: * Sc2tog; rep from * around—18 sts.

18th rnd: Rep 13th rnd.

19th rnd: * 2 sc in next st; rep from * around—36 sts.

20th–23rd rnds: Rep 13th rnd.

24th rnd: * Sc in next 4 sc, sc2tog; rep from * around—30 sts.

Fasten off.

Join: Stuff Cone and Ice Cream. With A, sew together. Sew 1st–9th rnds of Ice Cream together lengthwise, curl down and sew in place.

Cuff

With A, ch 5.

1st row: Sc in 2nd ch from hook and in each ch across; turn—4 sts.

2nd–28th rows: Ch 1, working in back loops ONLY, sc in each st across; turn.

FINISHING

Fasten off. Sew in place around top of Cone. Weave in ends. •

Little Piggy

Easy

MEASUREMENT
Pig measures 5½"/14cm tall.

MATERIALS
Yarn
Red Heart® Super Saver® Stripes™, 5oz/141g balls; each 236yd/215m (acrylic)
- 1 ball in #0722 Pretty 'n Pink (A)
- 1 ball in #0579 Pale Plum (B)

Hook
- Size F/5 (3.75mm) crochet hook, *or size needed to obtain gauge*

Notions
- Split-lock stitch marker
- Yarn needle
- Stuffing
- Two ¼"/0.5cm black buttons for eyes

GAUGE
16 sts and 20 rnds = 4"/10cm in single crochet using size F/5 (3.75mm) hook. *TAKE TIME TO CHECK GAUGE.*

STITCH GLOSSARY
dec (decrease) Draw up a loop in each of next 2 sc, yarn over and draw through all 3 loops on hook—1 stitch decreased.
inc (increase) 2 sc in next stitch.

NOTE
- Work in continuous rounds of sc without joining unless otherwise indicated. Place a marker in first stitch of round and move up each round.

HEAD AND BODY
Begin at top of Head with A, ch 2.
1st rnd: 6 Sc in 2nd ch from hook.
2nd rnd: 2 Sc in each sc around—12 sc.
3rd rnd: [Sc in next sc, inc] 6 times—18 sc.
4th rnd: [Sc in next 2 sc, inc] 6 times—24 sc.
5th rnd: [Sc in next 3 sc, inc] 6 times—30.
6th–12th rnds: Sc in each sc around.
13th rnd: [Dec] 15 times—15 sc.

Neck
14th rnd: [Sc in next 3 sc, dec] 3 times changing to B in last sc—12 sc.

Body
15th rnd: With B, [inc] 12 times—24 sc.
Stuff head.
16th–19th rnds: With B, sc in each sc around changing to A in last sc of Rnd 19.
20th rnd: With A, sc in back loops only of each sc around.
21st–24th rnds: Sc in each sc around.
Stuff body.
25th rnd: [Dec] 12 times—12 sc.
26th rnd: [Dec] 6 times—6 sc.
Fasten off. Finish stuffing. Weave yarn tail through remaining 6 sc, draw up firmly to gather together; fasten securely.

SKIRT
Join B in any back loop left unworked on Rnd 20; ch 2, 2 hdc in same loop as joining, 3 hdc in each loop around; join with a slip st in top of ch-2.
Fasten off.

SNOUT

With A, ch 2.

1st rnd: 6 Sc in 2nd ch from hook.

2nd rnd: 2 Sc in each sc around—12 sc.

3rd rnd: Sc in back loops only of each sc around.

4th rnd: Slip st in each sc around. Fasten off. Stuff lightly and sew in place.

Sew eyes in place above snout.

ARMS (MAKE 2)

With A, ch 2.

1st rnd: 6 Sc in 2nd ch from hook.

2nd rnd: [Sc in next sc, inc] 3 times—9 sc.

3rd–6th rnds: Sc in each sc around.

Fasten off

Stuff and sew in place.

LEGS (MAKE 2)

With A, ch 2.

1st rnd: 6 Sc in 2nd ch from hook.

2nd rnd: 2 Sc in each sc around—12 sc.

3rd–5th rnds: Sc in each sc around.

6th rnd: [Sc in next 2 sc, dec] 3 times—9 sc.

Fasten off. Stuff lightly and sew in place.

TAIL

With A, ch 6; 2 sc in 2nd ch from hook and in each ch across. Fasten off. Sew in place.

EARS (MAKE 2)

With A, ch 6.

1st row: Sc in 2nd ch from hook and in each ch across; turn—5 sc.

2nd and 4th rows: Ch 1, sc in each sc across; turn.

3rd row: Ch 1, dec, sc in next sc, dec; turn—3 sc.

5th row: Ch 1, draw up a loop in each of next 3 sc, yarn over and draw through all 4 loops on hook; turn—1 sc.

6th row: Ch 1, sc in sc, slip st in center st of 2nd row for ear fold.

FINISHING

Fasten off. Sew in place as pictured. •

35

Love My Giraffe

Easy

MEASUREMENT
Toy measures 21"/53cm tall.

MATERIALS
Yarn

Red Heart® With Love®, 7oz/198g balls, each approx 370yd/338m (acrylic)
- 1 ball in #1201 Daffodil (A)
- 1 ball in #1321 Chocolate (B)
- 1 ball in #1012 Black (C)

Hook
- Size I/9 (5.5mm) crochet hook, *or size needed to obtain gauge*

Notions
- Stuffing
- Safety eyes (optional)
- Stitch marker
- Yarn needle

GAUGE
11 sc = 3"/7.5cm; 14 rnds = 4"/10cm in sc using size I/9 (5.5mm) hook. *TAKE TIME TO CHECK GAUGE.*

HEAD
Beginning at top of Head, with A, ch 2.

1st rnd: 6 sc in 2nd ch from hook. Place marker for beginning of round.

2nd rnd: Working in continuous rounds, 2 sc in each sc around—12 sc.

3rd rnd: [Sc in next sc, 2 sc in next sc] around—18 sc.

4th rnd: [Sc in next 2 sc, 2 sc in next sc] around—24 sc.

5th rnd: [Sc in next 3 sc, 2 sc in next sc] around—30 sc.

6th rnd: [Sc in next 4 sc, 2 sc in next sc] around—36 sc.

7th–13th rnds: Sc in each sc around.

14th rnd: [Sc in next 10 sc, sc2tog] around—33 sc.

15th rnd: Sc in each sc around.

16th rnd: [Sc in next 9 sc, sc2tog] around—30 sc.

17th rnd: Sc in each sc around.

18th rnd: [Sc2tog] 6 times, sc in next 6 sc, 2 sc in next 6 sc, sc in next 6 sc—30 sc.

19th and 20th rnds: Sc in each sc around.

21st rnd: [Sc in next 3 sc, sc2tog] around—24 sc.

22nd rnd: Sc in each sc around.

23rd rnd: [Sc in next 2 sc, sc2tog] around—18 sc. Stuff Head with fiberfill.

24th rnd: Sc in each sc around.

25th rnd: [Sc in next sc, sc2tog] around—12 sc.

26th rnd: [Sc2tog] around—6 sc.

Fasten off. Cut yarn, leaving a long tail. Stuff Head. Weave tail through remaining sts and pull to gather sts to close. If using safety eyes, attach to face before closing Head.

EARS (MAKE 2)
With A, ch 2.

1st rnd: 6 sc in 2nd ch from hook. Place marker for beginning of round.

2nd rnd: Working in continuous rounds, [sc in next 2 sc, 2 sc in next sc] around—8 sc.

3rd rnd: Sc in each sc around.

4th rnd: [Sc in next sc, 2 sc in next sc] around—12 sc.

5th rnd: Sc in each sc around.

6th rnd: [Sc in next 2 sc, 2 sc in next sc] around—18 sc.

7th–9th rnds: Sc in each sc around.

10th rnd: [Sc2tog] around—9 sc.

11th rnd: Sc in each sc around.

Fasten off. Cut yarn, leaving a long tail. Flatten and sew an Ear on either side of Head.

Love My Giraffe

HORNS (MAKE 2)

With B, ch 2.

1st rnd: 6 sc in 2nd ch from hook. Place marker for beginning of round.

2nd rnd: Working in continuous rounds, 2 sc in each sc around—12 sc.

3rd rnd: Sc in each sc around.

4th rnd: Working in back loops only, [sc2tog] around—6 sc.

5th and 6th rnds: Sc in each sc around.

Fasten off. Cut yarn, leaving a long tail. Stuff with fiberfill. Sew Horns on Head in between Ears.

NECK AND BODY

Beginning at top of Neck and leaving a long tail, with A, ch 24, slip st in first ch to form a ring.

1st rnd: Ch 1, sc in same st as join and each ch around—24 sc. Place marker for beginning of round.

2nd–24th rnds: Working in continuous rounds, sc in each sc around.

25th rnd: [Sc in next 3 sc, 2 sc in next sc] around—30 sc.

26th rnd: Sc in next 12 sc, 2 sc in next 6 sc, sc in next 12 sc—36 sc.

27th and 28th rnds: Sc in each sc around.

29th rnd: Sc in next 15 sc, 2 sc next 6 sc, sc in next 15 sc—42 sc.

30th and 31st rnds: Sc in each sc around.

32 rnd: Sc in next 18 sc, 2 sc in next 6 sc, sc in next 18 sc—48 sc.

33rd–42nd rnds: Sc in each sc around.

43rd rnd: [Sc in next 6 sc, sc2tog] around—42 sc.

44th rnd: [Sc in next 5 sc, sc2tog] around—36 sc.

45th rnd: [Sc in next 4 sc, sc2tog] around—30 sc.

46th rnd: [Sc in next 3 sc, sc2tog] around—24 sc. Stuff Neck and Body.

47th rnd: [Sc in next 2 sc, sc2tog] around—18 sc.

48th rnd: [Sc in next sc, sc2tog] around—12 sc.

Fasten off. Cut yarn, leaving a long tail. Insert fiberfill firmly. Using long tail, sew Neck and Body closed.

LEGS (MAKE 4)

With C, ch 2.

1st rnd: 6 sc in 2nd ch from hook. Place marker for beginning of round.

2nd rnd: Working in continuous rounds, 2 sc in each sc around—12 sc.

3rd rnd: [Sc in next sc, 2 sc in next sc] around—18 sc.

4th and 5th rnds: Sc in each sc around. Cut C.

6th–17th rnds: Change to A, sc in each sc around. Fasten off. Cut yarn, leaving a long tail. Stuff Legs.

FINISHING

Embroider a few loop stitches with A in between Horns on Head. With C, embroider eyes and nostrils in satin stitch. Embroider mouth in couched stitch. Positioning Head to look towards one side, sew Neck to Head. Sew Legs to Body.

Mane

With B, ch 35.

1st row: Dc in 4th ch from hook, skip 3 sts, *7 dc in next st, skip 3 sts; rep from * to last st, sc in last st. Fasten off. Cut yarn, leaving a long tail. Sew Mane down center of Head and Neck.

Spots (Make 12)

With B, ch 2.

1st rnd: 6 sc in 2nd ch from hook. Place marker for beginning of round.

2nd rnd: Working in continuous rounds, 2 sc in each sc around, slip st in first st to join.

Fasten off. Sew Spots randomly around Body.

Tail

With A, ch 9, slip st in 2nd ch from hook and each ch across.

FINISHING

Fasten off. Cut yarn, leaving a long tail.

Cut four lengths of B, each 10"/25cm long. Thread each length through one end of Tail and center each length. Tie an overhand knot in lengths to secure and trim. Sew opposite end of tail to Body. Weave in ends. •

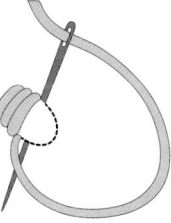

SATIN STITCH

Gnome Family

Easy

MEASUREMENT
Each gnome measures 8"/20cm tall, including Cap

MATERIALS
Yarn

Red Heart® Super Saver®, 7oz/198g balls, each approx 364yd/215m (acrylic)
- 1 ball in #0312 Black (A)
- 1 ball in #0319 Cherry Red (B)
- 1 ball in #0886 Blue (C)
- 1 ball in #0321 Gold (D)
- 1 ball in #0334 Buff (E)
- 1 ball in #0313 Aran (F)
- 1 ball in #0358 Lavender (G)
- 1 ball in #0512 Turqua (H)
- 1 ball in #0672 Spring Green (I)

Hook
- Size H/8 (5mm) crochet hook, *or size needed to obtain gauge*

Notions
- Yarn needle
- Stitch marker
- Stuffing
- One pair 6mm safety eyes

GAUGE
14 sts and 15 rows = 4"/10cm in single crochet using size H/8 (5mm) hook. *TAKE TIME TO CHECK GAUGE.*

STITCH GLOSSARY
3-hdc popcorn 3 hdc in indicated stitch, remove hook from loop, insert hook from front to back in first hdc of 3-hdc group, place dropped loop back on hook and draw through.

SPECIAL TECHNIQUE
Adjustable ring Holding the yarn a few inches from the end, wrap around your finger. Do not remove wrap from finger, insert hook into the wrap and draw up a loop of working yarn. Chain one to secure the loop, and remove ring from finger. Work stitches of first round in the ring. Pull gently, but firmly, on tail to tighten ring.

NOTES
- Only small amounts of each color are needed. Many gnomes can be made from 1 skein of each color.
- When fastening off at the end of a round. You may wish to finish with an invisible join, as follows: Cut yarn, leaving a long tail. Pull up on last loop on hook until tail is drawn all the way through the last stitch. Thread tail onto yarn needle. Insert yarn needle under both strands of 2nd stitch of round, then insert needle down through last stitch. This creates a loop that looks like the top of a stitch. Weave in the remaining tail.
- Stuff pieces lightly. Do not over stuff.
- Gauge is not critical. Work tightly to ensure that stuffing does not show through stitches.

PAPA
Legs (Make 2)

Beginning at shoe, with A, make an adjustable ring.

1st rnd: (RS) Work (3 sc, 2 hdc, 3 sc) in ring; join with slip st in first sc—8 sts.

2nd rnd: Ch 1, sc in first 3 sc, 2 hdc in each of next 2 hdc (for toe), sc in last 3 sc; join with slip st in first sc—10 sts.

3rd rnd: Ch 1, sc in each st around; join with slip st in first sc.

4th rnd: Ch 1, sc in first 3 sc, [sc2tog] 2 times, sc in last 3 sc; join with slip st in first sc—8 sc.
Fasten off.

41

Gnome Family

5th rnd: With Right Side facing, join B with sc in first sc of 4th rnd, sc in each remaining sc around; do not join, work in continuous rounds. Place marker for beginning of round. Move marker up as each round is completed.

6th and 7th rnds: Sc in each sc around.

8th rnd: [Sc in next 3 sc, 2 sc in next sc] 2 times—10 sc. Fasten off. Hold both legs together, with toes facing in the same direction. Sew tops of legs together, sewing through 2 stitches at inside of each leg and leaving 8 stitches on each leg unsewn. Stuff legs.

Lower Tunic

With C, ch 24; taking care not to twist ch, join with slip st in first ch to form a ring.

1st rnd: (RS) Ch 1, sc in each ch around; do not join, work in continuous rounds—24 sc. Place marker for beginning of round. Move marker up as work progresses.

2nd rnd: [Sc in next 4 sc, sc2tog] 4 times—20 sc.

3rd rnd: Sc in next sc; place tunic around top of legs, beginning at back of legs, working through both thicknesses, sc in 8 unsewn sts of first leg; working in tunic sts only, sc in next 2 sc; working through both thicknesses, sc in 8 unsewn sts of 2nd leg; working in last tunic st only, sc in last sc—20 sc. Fasten off.

Belt

1st rnd: Join A with sc at center back of tunic, sc in each remaining sc around; join with slip st in first sc. Fasten off.

Upper Tunic

1st rnd: Join C with sc at center back of belt, sc in each sc around; do not join, work in continuous rounds. Place marker for beginning of round. Move marker up as work progresses.

2nd and 3rd rnds: Sc in each sc around.

4th rnd: Sc in next 4 sc, [sc2tog] twice, sc in next 6 sc, [sc2tog] twice, sc in next 2 sc—16 sc.

5th rnd: [Sc2tog] 8 times—8 sc. Stuff tunic. Fasten off, leaving a long tail for sewing tunic to head. With D, embroider a straight stitch square on center, front of belt for buckle.

Arms (Make 2)

Beginning at hand, with E, make an adjustable ring.

1st rnd: (RS) Work 8 sc in ring; do not join, work in continuous rounds—8 sc. Place marker for beginning of round. Move marker up as work progresses.

2nd rnd: Sc in each sc around.

3rd rnd: [Sc in next 2 sc, sc2tog] 2 times—6 sc. Fasten off.

Sleeve

4th rnd: Join C with sc in first sc of 3rd rnd, sc in next 5 sc.

5th–8th rnds: Sc in each sc around. Do not stuff arm.

9th rnd: [Sc2tog] 3 times—3 sc.

Fasten off, leaving a long tail for sewing arm to tunic.

Head

With E, make an adjustable ring.

1st rnd: (RS) Work 6 sc in ring; do not join, work in continuous rounds—6 sc. Place marker for beginning of round. Move marker up as work progresses.

2nd rnd: Work 2 sc in each sc around—12 sc.

3rd rnd: [Sc in next sc, 2 sc in next sc] 6 times—18 sc.

4th and 5th rnds: Sc in each sc around.

6th rnd: Sc in next 9 sc, 3-hdc popcorn in next sc (for nose), sc in last 8 sc.

7th rnd: Sc in each sc around. Attach safety eyes, between 5th and 6th rnds, on either side of nose.

Note: Push posts of safety eyes between strands of a stitch, not in space between stitches, to avoid allowing the eye to sink back into the head.

8th rnd: [Sc in next sc, sc2tog] 6 times—12 sc.

9th rnd: [Sc in next sc, sc2tog] 4 times—8 sc.

10th rnd: Sc in each sc around.

Fasten off. Stuff head.

Cap

With B, make an adjustable ring.

1st rnd: (RS) Work 4 sc in ring; do not join, work in continuous rounds—4 sc. Place marker for beginning of round. Move marker up as work progresses.

2nd rnd: Sc in each sc around.

3rd rnd: Work 2 sc in each sc around—8 sc.

4th rnd: Sc in each sc around.

5th rnd: [Sc in next sc, 2 sc in next sc] 4 times—12 sc.

6th rnd: Sc in each sc around.

7th rnd: [Sc in next 2 sc, 2 sc in next sc] 4 times—16 sc.

8th rnd: Sc in each sc around.

9th rnd: [Sc in next 3 sc, 2 sc in next sc] 4 times—20 sc.

10th and 11th rnds: Sc in each sc around.

Fasten off.

Hair and Beard

1st row: With F, [ch 3, working in back bars, slip st in 2nd ch from hook and in next ch] 4 times, [ch 4, working in back bars, slip st in 2nd ch from hook and in next 2 ch] 4 times, [ch 5, working in back bars, slip st in 2nd ch from hook and in next 3 ch] 2 times, [ch 4, working in back bars, slip st in 2nd ch from hook and in next 2 ch] 4 times, [ch 3, working in back bars, slip st in 2nd ch from hook and in next ch] 4 times.

Fasten off, leaving a long tail for sewing hair and beard to cap and face.

Front Curl (Optional)

With F, ch 5, working in back bars, slip st in 3rd ch from hook and in next 2 ch.

Fasten off, leaving a long tail for sewing curl to underside of cap.

Mustache

With F, [ch 5, slip st in 2nd ch from hook and in next 3 ch] 2 times.

Fasten off, leaving a long tail for sewing mustache to face.

FINISHING

Sew arms to sides of body, near top of tunic. Sew head to top of tunic. Sew front curl to underside of center front of cap. Sew ends of hair and beard piece together to form a ring. Sew piece to underside of cap edge, placing seam centered at back of cap, and sewing for about ½"/1cm on each side of seam (to about where ears would be). Place cap on head and sew in place. Arrange beard around chin and sides of face and sew in place. Sew mustache beneath nose. Weave in all ends.

BOY

Legs (Make 2)

Work same as papa's legs through 7th rnd, using A for shoe and D for legs. Work one more round, as follows, before finishing leg.

8th rnd: Sc in each sc around.

9th rnd: [Sc in next 3 sc, 2 sc in next sc] 2 times—10 sc.

Fasten off. Hold both legs together, with toes facing in the same direction. Sew tops of legs together, sewing through 2 stitches at inside of each leg and leaving 8 stitches on each leg unsewn. Stuff legs.

Gnome Family

Lower Tunic

With I, ch 20; taking care not to twist ch, join with slip st in first ch to form a ring.

1st rnd: Ch 1, sc in each ch around; join with slip st in first sc.

Fasten off.

Belt

1st rnd: Place tunic around top of legs, join A with sc in first sc of belt, beginning at back of legs, working through both thicknesses, sc in 8 unsewn sts of first leg, sc in next 2 sc of belt only, working through both thicknesses, sc in 8 unsewn sts of 2nd leg, sc in last sc of belt; join with slip st in first sc—20 sc.

2nd rnd: Sc in each sc around; join with slip st in first sc.

Fasten off.

Upper Tunic

With I, work same as papa's upper tunic.

Arms (Make 2)

Work same as papa's arm, using E for hand, and I for sleeve.

Head

Work same as papa's head.

Cap

With C, work same as papa's cap.

Hair

1st row: With A, [ch 3, working in back bars, slip st in 2nd ch from hook and in next ch] 18 times.

Fasten off, leaving a long tail for sewing hair to cap. Sew last stitch to first stich. Sew hair to underside of cap edge.

FINISHING

Sew arms to sides of body, near top of tunic. Sew head to top of tunic. Sew cap to top of head. With B, embroider straight stitch mouth below nose.

GIRL

Legs (Make 2)

Work same as boy's legs, using G for shoe and E for leg.

Skirt

With I, ch 48; taking care not to twist ch, join with slip st in first ch.

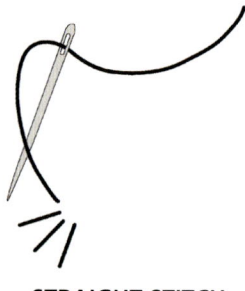

STRAIGHT STITCH

1st rnd: (ruffle) Taking care not to twist ch, sc in first ch., sc in next ch, skip next 2 ch, [sc in next 2 ch, skip next 2 ch] 11 times; do not join, work in continuous rounds—24 sc. Place marker for beginning of round. Move marker up as work progresses.
2nd and 3rd rnds: Sc in each sc around.
4th rnd: Sc in next 5 sc, sc2tog, sc in next 10 sc, sc2tog, sc in next 5 sc—22 sc.
5th rnd: Sc in next 5 sc, sc2tog, sc in next 9 sc, sc2tog, sc in next 4 sc—20 sc.
Fasten off.

Waistband

1st rnd: Place skirt around top of legs, join H with sc in first sc of waistband, beginning at back of legs, working through both thicknesses, sc in 8 unsewn sts of first leg, sc in next 2 sc of waistband only, working through both thicknesses, sc in 8 unsewn sts of 2nd leg, sc in last sc of waistband; join with slip st in first sc—20 sc.
Fasten off.

Blouse

With G, work same as papa's upper tunic.
Arms (Make 2) Work same as papa's arm, using E for hand and G for sleeve.

Head

Work same as papa's head.

Cap

Work same as papa's cap.

Hair

With D, [ch 10, 3 sc in 2nd ch from hook, 3 sc in each of next 4 ch, sc in next 4 ch] 5 times, [ch 3, slip st in 2nd ch from hook and next ch] 5 times (for bangs), [ch 10, 3 sc in 2nd ch from hook, 3 sc in each of next 4 ch, sc in next 4 ch] 5 times.
Fasten off, leaving a long tail for sewing hair to cap. Sew last stitch to first stitch. Sew hair to underside of cap edge, centering bangs at front of cap.

FINISHING

Sew arms to sides of body, near top of blouse. Sew head to top of blouse. Sew cap to top of head. With B, embroider straight stitch mouth below nose. •

Squish-a-Saurus

Designed by Sarah Zimmerman (Repeat Crafter Me)

Easy

MEASUREMENT
Approx 12½"/32cm tall

MATERIALS
Yarn
Red Heart® Super Saver®, 7oz/198g balls, each approx 364yd/215m (acrylic)
- 1 ball in #0672 Spring Green (A)
- 1 ball in #0368 Paddy Green (B)

Hook
- Size H/8 (5mm) crochet hook, *or size needed to obtain gauge*

Notions
- Stuffing
- Two 5mm safety eyes
- Tapestry needle

GAUGE
13 sc and 15 rows = 4"/10cm using size H/8 (5mm) hook. *TAKE TIME TO CHECK GAUGE.*

NOTE
- All rnds are joined with a sl st to first st. Ch 2 at beg of rnd does not count as st.

FEET (MAKE 2)
With A, beg using magic loop method, demonstrated here.

1st rnd: Ch 1. 6 sc in ring. Join.

2nd rnd: Ch 2. 2 dc in each of next 2 sts. 2 hdc in each of next 2 sts. 2 sc in each of next 2 sts. Join. 12 sts.

3rd rnd: Ch 1. 2 sc in each st around. Join. 24 sts.

4th and 5th rnds: Ch 1. 1 sc in each st around. Join.

6th rnd: Ch 1. (Sc2tog) 5 times. 1 sc in each of the last 14 sts. Join. 19 sts.

7th rnd: Ch 1. 1 sc in each st around. Join.

8th rnd: Ch 1. (Sc2tog) 3 times. 1 sc in each of last 13 sts. Join. 16 sts.

9th–12th rnds: Ch 1. 1 sc in each st around. Join. Fasten off.

ARMS (MAKE 2)
With A, beg using magic loop method.

1st rnd: Ch 1. 6 sc in ring. Join.

2nd rnd: Ch 2. 2 sc in each st around. Join. 12 sts.

3rd rnd: Ch 1. *2 sc in next st. 1 sc in next st. Rep from * around. Join. 18 sts.

4th–6th rnds: Ch 1. 1 sc in each st around. Join.

7th rnd: Ch 1. *Sc2tog. 1 sc in each of next 4 sts. Rep from * around. Join. 15 sts.

8th rnd: Ch 1. 1 sc in each st around. Join.

9th rnd: Ch 1. *Sc2tog. 1 sc in each of next 3 sts. Rep from * around. Join. 12 sts.

10th to 17th rnds: As 8th rnd. Fasten off.

SPIKES (MAKE 6)
With B, beg using magic loop method.

1st rnd: Ch 1. 4 sc in ring. Join.

2nd rnd: Ch 1. (2 sc in next st. 1 sc in next st) twice. Join. 6 sts.

3rd rnd: Ch 1. (2 sc in next st. 1 sc in each of next 2 sts) twice. Join. 8 sts.

4th rnd: Ch 1. (2 sc in next st. 1 sc in each of next 3 sts) twice. Join. 10 sts.

5th rnd: Ch 1. (2 sc in next st. 1 sc in each of next 4 sts) twice. Join. 12 sts.

6th rnd: Ch 1. (2 sc in next st. 1 sc in each of next 5 sts) twice. Join. 14 sts.

7th rnd: Ch 1. (2 sc in next st. 1 sc in each of next 6 sts) twice. Join. 16 sts. Fasten off.

Squish-a-Saurus

TAIL

With A, beg using magic loop method.

1st rnd: Ch 1. 4 sc in ring. Join.

2nd rnd: Ch 1. *2 sc in next st. 1 sc in next st. Rep from * around. Join. 6 sts.

3rd and alt rnds: Ch 1. 1 sc in each st around. Join.

4th rnd: Ch 1. *2 sc in next st. 1 sc in each of next 2 sts. Rep from * around. Join. 8 sts.

6th rnd: Ch 1. *2 sc in next st. 1 sc in each of next 3 sts. Rep from * around. Join. 10 sts.

8th rnd: Ch 1. *2 sc in next st. 1 sc in each of next 4 sts. Rep from * around. Join. 12 sts.

10th rnd: Ch 1. *2 sc in next st. 1 sc in each of next 5 sts. Rep from * around. Join. 14 sts.

12th rnd: Ch 1. *2 sc in next st. 1 sc in each of next 6 sts. Rep from * around. Join. 16 sts.

14th rnd: Ch 1. *2 sc in next st. 1 sc in each of next 7 sts. Rep from * around. Join. 18 sts.

16th rnd: Ch 1. *2 sc in next st. 1 sc in each of next 8 sts. Rep from * around. Join. 20 sts.

18th rnd: As 6th rnd. 25 sts.

20th rnd: As 8th rnd. 30 sts.

22nd rnd: As 4th rnd.

23rd rnd: As 3rd rnd. Fasten off.

BODY

With A, beg using magic loop method.

1st rnd: Ch 1. 10 sc in ring. Join.

2nd rnd: Ch 2. 2 sc in each st around. Join. 20 sts.

3rd rnd: Ch 1. *2 sc in next st. 1 sc in next st. Rep from * around. Join. 30 sts.

4th rnd: Ch 1. 1 sc in each st around. Join.

5th rnd: Ch 1. * 2 sc in next st. 1 sc in each of next 2 sts. Rep from * around. Join. 40 sts.

6th rnd: Ch 1. * 2 sc in next st. 1 sc in each of next 3 sts. Rep from * around. Join. 50 sts.

7th rnd: As 4th rnd.

8th rnd: Ch 1. * 2 sc in next st. 1 sc in each of next 4 sts. Rep from * around. Join. 60 sts.

9th–13th rnds: As 4th rnd.

14th rnd: Ch 1. *Sc2tog. 1 sc in each of next 4 sts. Rep from * around. Join. 50 sts.

15th–18th rnds: As 4th rnd.

19th rnd: Ch 1. *Sc2tog. 1 sc in each of next 3 sts. Rep from * around. Join. 40 sts.

20th–22nd rnd: As 4th rnd.

23rd rnd: Ch 1. *Sc2tog. 1 sc in each of next 2 sts. Rep from * around. Join. 30 sts.

24th–29th rnds: As 4th rnd.

30th rnd: Ch 1. *Sc2tog. 1 sc in next st. Rep from * around. Join. 20 sts.

31st–34th rnds: As 4th rnd. Fasten off, leaving a long tail. Stuff body, leaving top open.

HEAD

With A, beg using magic loop method.

1st rnd: Ch 1. 10 sc in ring. Join.

2nd rnd: Ch 2. 2 sc in each st around. Join. 20 sts.

3rd rnd: Ch 1. 1 sc in each st around. Join.

4th rnd: Ch 1. *2 sc in next st. 1 sc in next st. Rep from * around. Join. 30 sts.

5th rnd: Ch 1. 1 sc in each st around. Join.

6th rnd: Ch 1. (2 sc in next st. 1 sc in each of next 2 sts) twice. Join. 40 sts.

7th rnd: Ch 1. (2 sc in next st. 1 sc in each of next 3 sts) twice. Join. 50 sts.

8th–11th rnds: As 3rd rnd.

12th rnd: Ch 1. *Sc2tog. 1 sc in each of next 3 sts. Rep from * around. Join. 40 sts.

Note: Safety eyes should be placed between 13th and 14th rnd, and should be spaced 10 sts apart as shown in photo. Begin stuffing Head as you work.

13th–15th rnds: As 3rd rnd.

16th rnd: Ch 1. *Sc2tog. 1 sc in each of next 2 sts. Rep from * around. Join. 30 sts.

17th–24th rnds: As 3rd rnd.

25th rnd: Ch 1. Sc2tog. 1 sc in next st. Rep from * around. Join. 20 sts.

26th rnd: As 3rd rnd.

27th rnd: Ch 1. *Sc2tog. Rep from * around. Join. 10 sts.

28th rnd: As 27th rnd. 5 sts.

Fasten off leaving a long end. Draw end tightly through rem sts and fasten securely.

FINISHING

Stuff Arms and Spikes and sew to Body as shown in photo. Sew Legs and Tail to body as shown in photo, stuffing as you work. Refer to tutorial video here for comprehensive finishing instructions. •

Happy Plane, Car & Truck

Easy

MEASUREMENTS
Car measures 2¾"/7cm wide x 4½"/11.5cm long.
Plane measures 8"/20.5cm long x 8"/20.5cm wide across wings.
Truck measures 2¾"/7cm wide x 7"/18cm long.

MATERIALS
Yarn
Red Heart® Super Saver®, 7oz/198g balls, each approx 364yd/215m (acrylic) [4]
- 1 ball in #0319 Cherry Red (A)
- 1 ball in #0324 Bright Yellow (B)
- 1 ball in #0316 Soft White (C)
- 1 ball in #0312 Black (D)
- 1 ball in #0400 Grey Heather (E)
- 1 ball in #0505 Aruba Sea (F)
- 1 ball in #0672 Spring Green (G)
- 1 ball in #0254 Pumpkin (H)
- 1 ball in #0886 Blue (I)

Hook
- Size F/5 (3.75mm) crochet hook, *or size needed to obtain gauge*

Notions
- Stuffing
- Yarn needle

GAUGE
15 sts and 16 rows/rnds = 4"/10cm in single crochet using size F/5 (3.75mm) hook. *TAKE TIME TO CHECK GAUGE.*

STITCH GLOSSARY
bpdc (back post double crochet) Yarn over, insert hook from back side of work to front and to back again around the post of indicated stitch; yarn over and pull up a loop (3 loops on hook), yarn over and draw through 2 loops (2 loops on hook), yarn over and draw through 2 loops (1 loop on hook). Skip the stitch in front of the bpdc.

fpdc (front post double crochet) Yarn over, insert hook from front side of work to back and to front again around post of indicated stitch; yarn over and pull up a loop (3 loops on hook), yarn over and draw through 2 loops (2 loops on hook), yarn over and draw through 2 loops (1 loop on hook).

NOTES
- Car, plane, and truck are worked in pieces that are sewn together.
- Sections worked in rounds have right sides facing at all times and are joined at the end of each round.
- To change color, work last stitch of old color to last yarn over. Yarn over with new color and draw through all loops on hook to complete stitch. Proceed with new color. Cut old color.
- Insert stuffing only when instructed.

CAR
Body
Beginning at front of car, with A, ch 8.
1st rnd: Work 3 sc in 2nd ch from hook, sc in next 5 ch, 3 sc in last ch; working across opposite side of foundation ch, sc in next 5 ch; join with slip st in first sc—16 sc.

2nd rnd: Ch 1, 2 sc in first 3 sc, sc in next 5 sc, 2 sc in next 3 sc, sc in remaining sc; join with slip st in first sc—22 sc.

3rd–16th rnds: Ch 1, sc in each sc around; join with slip st in first sc.

17th rnd: Ch 1, sc in first 3 sc, sc2tog 3 times, sc in next 5 sc, sc2tog 3 times, sc in last 2 sc; join with slip st in first sc—16 sc.

18th rnd: Ch 1, sc in first 3 sc, sc3tog, sc in next 5 sc, sc3tog, sc in last 2 sc; join with slip st in first sc—12 sc. Fasten off, leaving long tail for sewing. Stuff lightly and, holding edges together, sew last round closed.

Roof

With A, ch 2.

1st rnd: Work 6 sc in 2nd ch from hook; join with slip st in first sc—6 sc.

2nd rnd: Ch 1, 2 sc in each st around; join with slip st in first sc—12 sc.

3rd rnd: Ch 1, [sc in next sc, 2 sc in next sc] 6 times; join with slip st in first sc—18 sc.

4th rnd: Ch 1, [sc in next 2 sc, 2 sc in next sc] 6 times; join with slip st in first sc—24 sc.

5th and 6th rnds: Ch 1, sc in each sc around; join with slip st in first sc.

Fasten off, leaving long tail for sewing. Stuff lightly, then sew roof over 8th–15th rnds of body.

Front and Rear Windows (Make 2)

With C, ch 7.

1st row: (RS) Sc in 2nd ch from hook and in each ch across, turn—6 sc.

2nd row: Ch 1, sc in each sc.

Fasten off, leaving long tail for sewing. With D, embroider straight st eyes over 3rd st from each edge of 1st row of front window. Sew front window over 5th and 6th rnds of front side of roof. Sew rear window over 5th and 6th rnds of back side of roof.

Happy Plane, Car & Truck

Side Windows (Make 2)

With C, ch 2.

1st row: (RS) Work 3 sc in 2nd ch from hook, turn—3 sc.

2nd row: Ch 1, 2 sc in each sc—6 sc.

Fasten off, leaving long tail for sewing. Sew side windows over 5th and 6th rnds of each side of roof.

Bumpers (Make 2)

With E, ch 15.

1st row: (RS) Sc in 2nd ch from hook and in each ch across—14 sc.

Fasten off, leaving long tail for sewing.

Headlights (Make 2)

With B, ch 2.

1st rnd: Work 5 sc in 2nd ch from hook; join with slip st in first sc—5 sc.

Fasten off leaving long tail for sewing.

Tire Halves (Make 8)

With E, ch 2.

1st rnd: Work 6 sc in 2nd ch from hook; join with slip st in first sc; change to D—6 sc.

2nd rnd: Ch 1, 2 sc in each sc around; join with slip st in first sc—12 sc.

Fasten off, leaving long tail on 4 tire halves for sewing. To form tire, *holding wrong sides together, whipstitch two tire halves around outer edges; rep from * 3 times.

ASSEMBLY

Sew bumpers over lower front and back of body, ensuring that each bumper is centered and wrapped slightly around each side. Using photograph as a guide, with D, backstitch curved mouth on front bumper. Sew headlights above ends of front bumper. Allow half of each tire to hang below body and sew in place on lower sides between edges of bumpers.

FINISHING CAR

Weave in ends.

PLANE

Nose and Body

Note: Insert stuffing every few rounds.

Beginning at nose, with F, ch 2.

1st rnd: Work 6 sc in 2nd ch from hook; join with slip st in first sc—6 sc.

2nd rnd: Ch 1, 2 sc in each st around; join with slip st in first sc—12 sc.

3rd rnd: Ch 1, sc in each sc around; join with slip st in first sc.

4th rnd: Ch 1, [sc in next sc, 2 sc in next sc] 6 times; join with slip st in first sc—18 sc.

5th and 6th rnds: Rep 3rd rnd; change to G at end of 6th rnd.

7th rnd: Ch 1, [sc in next 2 sc, 2 sc in next sc] 6 times; join with slip st in first sc—24 sc.

8th rnd: Ch 1, [sc in next 3 sc, 2 sc in next sc] 6 times, sc in remaining sc; join with slip st in first sc—30 sc.

9th rnd: Rep 3rd rnd.

10th rnd: Ch 1, [sc in next 3 sc, sc2tog] 6 times—24 sc.

11th–19th rnds: Rep 3rd rnd nine times.

20th rnd: Ch 1, [sc in next 2 sc, sc2tog] 6 times—18 sc.

21st–26th rnds: Rep 3rd rnd six times.

27th rnd: Ch 1, [sc in next sc, sc2tog] 6 times—12 sc.

28th–31st rnds: Rep 3rd rnd four times.

32nd rnd: Ch 1, sc2tog around; join with slip st in first sc—6 sc.

33rd rnd: Rep 3rd rnd.

Fasten off, leaving a long tail. Weave end through last sts and pull tightly to close tail end of body. On underside of nose, with D, embroider curved smile with backstitches between 3rd and 4th rnds.

Front Wings (Make 2)

Beginning at outer tip of wing, with H, ch 8.

1st row: (RS) Sc in 2nd ch from hook and in each ch across, turn—7 sc.

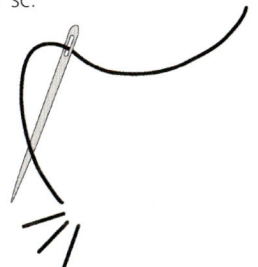

STRAIGHT STITCH

2nd row: Ch 1, sc in each sc, turn.

3rd row: Ch 1, sc in first 3 sc, 3 sc in next sc, sc in remaining sc, turn—9 sc.

4th row: Ch 1, sc in each sc, turn.

5th row: Ch 1, sc in each sc to center st of 3-sc group, 3 sc in center st, sc in remaining sc, turn—11 sc.

6th–13th rows: Rep Rows 4 and 5 four times—19 sc.

14 row: Rep 4th row.

Fasten off, leaving long tail for sewing. Fold wing in half lengthwise and whipstitch outer edges together.

Rear Wings (Make 3)

Beginning at outer tip of wing, with H, ch 6.

1st row: (RS) Sc in 2nd ch from hook and in each ch across, turn— 5 sc.

2nd row: Ch 1, sc in each sc, turn.

3rd row: Ch 1, sc in first 2 sc, 3 sc in next sc, sc in remaining sc, turn—7 sc.

4th row: Rep 2nd row.

Happy Plane, Car & Truck

5th row: Ch 1, sc in first 3 sc, 3 sc in next sc, sc in remaining sc, turn—9 sc.

6th row: Rep 2nd row.

Fasten off, leaving long tail for sewing. Fold wing in half lengthwise and whipstitch outer edges together.

Windshield

With C, ch 7.

1st row: (RS) Sc in 2nd ch from hook and in each ch across, turn—6 sc.

2nd row: Ch 1, 2 sc in each sc—12 sc.

Fasten off leaving long tail. With D, embroider straight st eyes 1 stitch apart from center of 1st row of windshield. Sew windshield over 7th and 8th rnds of body.

Front Tire Halves (Make 4)

With E, ch 2.

1st rnd: Work 6 sc in 2nd ch from hook; join with slip st in first sc; change to D—6 sc.

2nd rnd: Ch 1, 2 sc in each sc; join with slip st in first sc—12 sc.

Fasten off, leaving long tail on 2 tire halves for sewing. Holding wrong sides together, whipstitch two tire halves around outer edges; rep for 2nd tire.

Rear Tire Halves (Make 2)

With D, ch 2.

1st rnd: Work 6 sc in 2nd ch from hook; join with slip st in first sc—6 sc.

Fasten off leaving long tail on 1 tire half for sewing. Holding wrong sides together, whipstitch tire halves around outer edges.

ASSEMBLY

Using photograph as a guide for placement, sew front wings on sides of body over 14th–20th rnds and 2 rear wings over 30th–33rd rnds. Sew remaining wing over top of body over 30th–33rd rnds. Sew front tires to underside of body slightly forward of front wings; sew rear tire to underside of body centered between rear wings. Weave in ends.

TRUCK

Cab Body

With I, ch 34.

1st row: (RS) Dc in 4th ch from hook (beginning ch-3 counts as first dc here and throughout), dc in each ch across, turn—32 dc.

2nd row: Ch 3, dc in first 3 dc, [bpdc around next dc, dc in next 7 dc] three times, bpdc around next dc, dc in next 3 dc, turn.

3rd row: Ch 3, dc in first 2 dc, [fpdc around next dc, dc in next 7 dc] three times, fpdc around next dc, dc in last 4 dc, turn.

4th and 5th rows: Rep Rows 2 and 3.

6th row: Rep 2nd row.

Fasten off, leaving long tail for sewing.

Cab Top and Bottom (Make 2)

With I, ch 2.

1st rnd: Work 8 sc in 2nd ch from hook; join with slip st in first sc—8 sc.

2nd rnd: Ch 1, (sc, ch 2, sc) in first sc, sc in next st, *(sc, ch 2, sc) in first sc, sc in next st; rep from * 3 times; join with slip st in first sc—12 sc and 4 ch-2 sps.

3rd rnd: Ch 1, sc in first sc, *(sc, ch 2, sc) in next ch-2 space, sc in next 3 sc; rep from * twice, (sc, ch 2, sc) in next ch-2 space, sc in last 2 sc; join with slip st in first sc—20 sc and 4 ch-2 sps.

4th rnd: Ch 1, sc in first 2 sc, *(sc, ch 2, sc) in next ch-2 space, sc in next 5 sc; rep from * twice, (sc, ch 2, sc) in next ch-2 space, sc in last 3 sc; join with slip st in first sc—28 sc and 4 ch-2 sps.

Fasten off leaving long tail for sewing.

Front Bumper

With E, ch 15.

1st row: (RS) Sc in 2nd ch from hook and in each ch across—14 sc.

Fasten off, leaving long tail for sewing.

Grill

With E, ch 5.

1st row: (RS) Sc in 2nd ch from hook and in each ch across, turn—4 sc.

2nd and 3rd rows: Ch 1, sc in each sc, turn.

Fasten off, leaving long tail for sewing.

Headlights (Make 2)

With B, ch 2.

1st rnd: Work 6 sc in 2nd ch from hook; join with slip st in first sc—6 sc.

Fasten off, leaving long tail for sewing.

Front Windshield

With C, ch 7.

1st row: (RS) Sc in 2nd ch from hook and in each ch across, turn—6 sc.

2nd row: Ch 1, sc in each sc.

Fasten off, leaving long tail for sewing. With D, embroider straight st eyes 1 stitch apart from center of 1st row of front windshield.

Side Windows (Make 2)

With C, ch 5.

1st row: (RS) Sc in 2nd ch from hook and in each ch across, turn—4 sc.

2nd row: Ch 1, sc in each sc.

Fasten off, leaving long tail for sewing.

Trailer Box Top and Bottom (Make 2)

With E, ch 19.

1st row: (RS) Sc in 2nd ch from hook and in each ch across, turn—18 sc.

2nd–8th rows: Ch 1, sc in each sc, turn.

Fasten off, leaving long tail for sewing.

Trailer Box Sides (Make 2)

With E, ch 19.

1st row: (RS) Sc in 2nd ch from hook and in each ch across; turn—18 sc.

2nd row: Ch 1, sc in each sc; change to B, turn.

3rd and 4th rows: Ch 1, sc in each sc; change to A at end of 4th row, turn.

5th and 6th rows: Ch 1, sc in each sc; change to E at end of 6th row, turn.

7th row: Ch 1, sc in each sc, turn.

8th row: Ch 1, sc in each sc.

Fasten off.

Trailer Back End

With E, work same as cab top.

Happy Plane, Car & Truck

Tire Halves (Make 12)
With E, ch 2.

1st rnd: Work 6 sc in 2nd ch from hook; join with slip st in first sc—6 sc.

2nd rnd: Ch 1, 2 sc in each sc around; change to D; join with slip st in first sc—12 sc.

3rd rnd: Ch 1, sc in first sc, 2 sc in next st, *sc in next sc, 2 sc in next st; rep from * around; join with slip st in first sc—18 sc.

Fasten off, leaving long tail on six of the tire halves.

*Holding wrong sides together, whipstitch two tire halves around outer edges; rep from * 5 times.

ASSEMBLY
Cab
With right side of cab body facing, gently fold cab body so post sts form outer corners; working across ends of rows, sew edges together to form back of cab body. Sew cab top and bottom to body and stuff body before closing edges. Center the bumper over lower front of cab body, wrapping slightly and evenly around each side and sew in place.

Using photograph as a guide, with D, embroider curved smile with backstitches on bumper. Center grill over bumper and sew in place. Sew headlights on each side of grill. Align 1st row of front windshield over 5th row of cab body front and sew piece in place. Align 1st row of each side windshield over 5th row of cab body sides and sew in place.

Trailer
Sew trailer box top to top edges of box sides and box bottom to bottom edges. Sew back end to back of trailer box. Stuff trailer box, then whipstitch to back of cab body. Using photograph as a guide, sew tires to lower sides of truck, allowing half of each tire to hang below cab body and trailer box.

FINISHING TRUCK
Weave in ends. •